FROM COUNT
TO CITY SUBURB

OLD CATTON

IN THE TWENTIETH CENTURY

by

MAIRE BOOTY AND GEORGE JEFFRIES

PUBLISHED BY OLD CATTON SOCIETY
2001

reprinted June 2001

© OLD CATTON SOCIETY
Charity Reg. No. 297591

Type set on Acorn Risc PC in Computer Concepts Impression Style

ISBN 0-9539998-0-7

Printed by Catton Print
13-14 Roundtree Close, Norwich, Norfolk NR7 8SX

FOREWORD

Maire Booty and George Jeffries have taken an active part in village life in Old Catton for many years. Now they have worked together to produce this account of our village in the twentieth century. Meticulous research both into archive material and oral history is here presented in an eminently readable text. The photographs reproduced from the archive of Old Catton Society add further interest.

The History of Old Catton which I published over twenty years ago was designed as an aid for students and emphasised the early history of the village. This new book provides information which is presented largely through the eyes of those who have lived here and is imbued throughout with a love for the place and its people.

I am honoured to have been asked to write this Foreword but the book will be seen by readers as its own best recommendation.

Mary Manning.

Mary Manning (President, Old Catton Society)

ACKNOWLEDGEMENTS

This book has been written as the culmination of a series of events each of which was complete in itself but each of which, in turn, led on to another unforeseen and unplanned event.

In 1983, after careful deliberation, the Broadland District Council agreed to create a Conservation Area in Old Catton which encompassed Catton Hall and its Park, all of Church Street and parts of Spixworth Road and George Hill. In the wake of this recognition of Old Catton as an area of historic interest, a group of public-minded villagers met to consider ways of protecting the village. Prominent amongst these were Jock Raffe, Eric Briscoe, Bill Catton and Mary Manning. The result of their endeavours was the launching of the Old Catton Society in January, 1984, with its stated aims of preserving, protecting and promoting Old Catton. The Society was soon vigorously applying its precepts when it successfully opposed the demolition of the Camellia House which formed part of Catton Hall. Other actions, such as helping to landscape the New Cemetery, followed and, in 1994, the Society was again moving to preserve an historic part of the village. Almost by chance we found ourselves purchasing the ornamental pond that had once formed the centre-piece of Catton Hall's formal gardens and was now superfluous to Norfolk County Council's requirements.

It was then realised that the older inhabitants with all their wealth of knowledge of the village's past, personalities such as Mrs Liddington, Mrs Bird and Mrs Plumb, were slipping away from us and that it was essential to collect memories of the old times whilst we had the chance. This project progressed slowly until we approached Derek James of the Evening News whose subsequent article generated over forty responses from people willing to pass on their memories. Photographs as well as recorded memories started to accumulate and our next move was to establish an archive to collate all this material.

Following on from this it was obviously desirable to show something of what we had been collecting to the general public, and especially the people of Old Catton. So, with the agreement of the Parish Council and with participation by other village organisations, we staged an all-day exhibition in the Village Hall in June, 1997. The success of this display was based largely on the photographic side of the archive and prompted us to contemplate some way of making available to the public the many pages of recorded memories now in our possession. We chose the small book option – and this is it! It is based on memories – and memories are fallible – so it may not be totally accurate. But without the time willingly given by the under-noted there would have been no book at all.

Our Contributors:-

Mrs Angela Addinson, Mrs Allison, Mr Frank Betts, Mrs Brenda Bevis, Mrs Brocklebank, Mrs Beryl Blyth, Mr Jim Booty, Miss Maire Booty, Mr Jimmy Boulter, Mr John Bunting, Mrs Gill Burrell, Mr Andrew Buxton, Mr Arthur Cannings, Mrs Daphne Cary, Mr H Clements, Mrs E Coleman, Mr George Cubitt, Mrs Sheila Currall, Mr Douglas Day, Miss Betty Davis, Mrs Doreen Earl, Mr Geoffrey Deller, Mrs Edwards, Mrs Margaret Fisher, Mrs Eileen Grant, Mr Jimmy Mandell-Hall, Mr Ted Hawes, Mrs Eileen Hodgson, Mr W G Holmes, Mr F W Howell, Mr Richard Jackson, Mr W H Kelter, Mr John Lane, Mrs Barbara Lockwood, Mrs Dora Martin, Mr D Mays, Mrs Agnes Palmer, Mrs D Plane, Mr Leslie Potter, Mr Austin Pye, Miss Norma Roll, Miss Rosemary Shimmens, Mr Frank Shorten, Mr O F Simkin, Miss Iris Tillett, Mrs Iris Whittaker, Mrs Rose Whittaker, Mrs Eileen Wilby, Mr Leslie Willis, Mr Dennis Woods, Mrs Jessie Worship, and Mrs Wright.

For background information we have also drawn upon 'A History of Old Catton' by I M Manning (in fact our President, Mrs Mary Manning), Trevor Nuthall's book 'New Catton – The Story of a Norwich Suburb' and 'The Auxiliary Hospitals in Norfolk, 1914-1919' compiled by Colonel C E Knight. We also made good use of the Church Street School's Log Book with the kind permission of the Headmaster, Mr R Jackson, and the record of the Parish Council's Minutes which were made available to us by the Parish Clerk, Mrs Sally Barber. Information on aviation matters was obtained from Huby Fairhead's 'Norfolk Airfields and Airstrips' and from Mrs Christine Armes, whilst Mr Richard Barham kindly made available to us the results of his researches into the 1908 murder.

We are greatly indebted to Brian Larkman for the preparation of the map on page 8, to the Society's archivist, Ray Jones, who undertook the task of type setting, and also to Graham and Laura Jones for their advice and assistance on word and image processing.

Maire Booty, George Jeffries

Old Catton, November 2000

CONTENTS

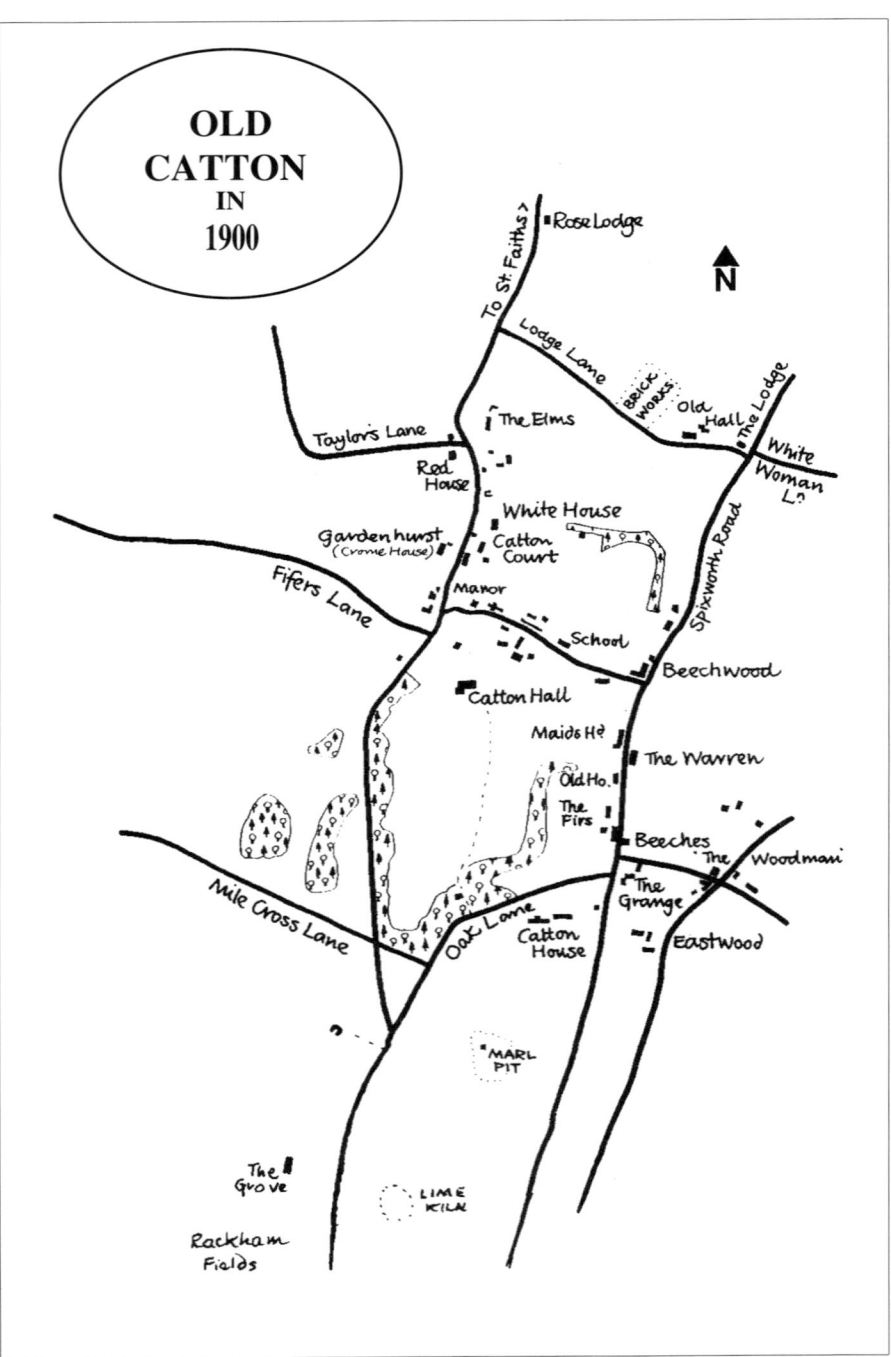

OLD CATTON IN 1900

INTRODUCTION

Old Catton stands on high ground just to the north of the Wensum Valley but, metaphorically speaking, the village has always stood in the shadow of its big neighbour. The City of Norwich spreads its influence throughout the village and, indeed, from the twelfth Century the Priors of the new Norwich Cathedral owned much of it and farmed the land well and profitably, handing it on to the Dean and Chapter of Norwich Cathedral at the Dissolution in 1538. This church patronage came to an end in 1780 when the Dean sold the Manor to Jeremiah Ives.

Norwich at this time was a prosperous and vibrant centre of the wool trade and the wealthy merchants were so imbued with success that they were moving out of the city in search of more ostentatious surroundings. Jeremiah Ives, a wealthy wool merchant of Colegate and twice Mayor of Norwich, came to Catton. There he built Catton Hall, guided by William Wilkins the architect, with its fine view of Norwich subsequently enhanced by the landscaping designs of Humphry Repton. He was followed in similar fashion by Thomas Harvey at Catton House, Robert Harvey at The Grange and Jeremiah Ives Harvey at Eastwood. This imported prosperity to the area, giving employment to estate workers, domestics and, soon, the ancillary trades of butcher, baker and beer-house. The merchants were augmented by an Admiral when, in 1814, Edward Berry settled in Spixworth Road at The Warren. He had been one of Nelson's favourite captains and had now retired. However, ill health forced him to move on to Bath in 1822.

Throughout the nineteenth Century this process continued and names familiar on the Norwich commercial scene took up residence in the quiet locations of Catton; the overall population continued to grow in response to the increasing opportunities for employment and by 1845 it was 650. St Margaret's Church which had changed only slowly over the centuries had, in turn, to respond to the expanding population and, under the enthusiastic direction of the Reverend Richard Hart, a new South Aisle and Pulpit were added in 1850 and a North Transept in 1861. A short way along Church Street a new school with two rooms and a village reading room was built in 1874 on land donated by the new owner of Catton Hall, Samuel Gurney Buxton; this was not only as a result of the growing insistence on primary education but also again because of the pressures of an expanding population.

In 1900, the professional men of Norwich were still finding Catton an attractive place of residence. Henry Carter, vintner, was at The Elms, Walter Overbury, solicitor, resided at The Firs and Arthur Bunting, clothier, occupied The Grange.

In addition, the rapidly growing population of Norwich had led to a great demand for locally grown fruit and vegetables and the whole of the land between Spixworth Road and North Walsham Road was dedicated to successful market gardens; Charles Betts and Ernest Hannent were described in Kelly's Directory as "Forced fruit growers". On the fringes of the village, beyond Lodge Lane and St Faiths Road, the land continued in conventional farming usage with its intensive labour and heavy machinery (ploughs and binders drawn by 3-horse teams). One of the major farmers here was Frank Gowing of Hellesdon Hall Farm. Service industries were also present with a small clutch of shops on the junction of George Hill and North Walsham Road where was also The Woodman public house; on Spixworth Road The Maids Head had been upgraded to full public house from the basic 'beer house' of the 1850s, whilst in Church Street a blacksmith, a saddler and a carpenter offered their services to the public as well as Catton Hall estate. Carters, wheelwrights and bricklayers were also available. The solitary intrusion of industry into this pastoral scene was the brickworks on Lodge Lane with its kiln, chimney, brick stacks and clay pits.

THE CAT ON THE BARREL

Village signs became very fashionable in the 1930s and many villages chose to erect theirs to commemorate either the Silver Jubilee of King George V in 1935, or the Coronation of George VI in 1937.

Our sign was designed and presented to the village by Mr Fred Gough, owner of the Norwich Paper and Cardboard Co. in Cowgate, Norwich, and resident of Crome House in St Faiths Road. He suggested the idea to the Parish Council in November, 1936, the offer was gratefully accepted and the resplendent sign was erected and unveiled by his son with due ceremony in June, 1937.

The motif for the sign was taken from the depiction of a cat and barrel carved on the timber frame of the door to the Manor House in Church Street; a similar rebus can be seen in the coloured glass of the west window, dating from 1870, of the village church.

At the outbreak of the Second World War, in 1939, village signs with all other identifying name plates were removed from their sites in order to "confuse the enemy in the event of invasion". The Old Catton sign was taken to a position outside the Officers' Mess on St Faiths Airfield where it remained throughout the war, becoming an object of some affection to the service personnel. So much so, perhaps, that on the 14th June, 1945, the Commanding Officer sent a letter to Old Catton Parish Council: "I regret to inform you that the cat is missing from your village sign". However, on this occasion, the cat was quickly traced to an RAF squadron that had taken him as a souvenir when they left and he returned to his perch later that month. The Parish Council was prompted by this incident to ask for the return of the sign from the airfield to its proper position at the Church Street junction, and this was accomplished in June, 1946.

Then, in August, 1950, Catton's cat disappeared again. Once more it was quickly traced to high-spirited airmen and the RAF not only returned it to the village but also kindly renovated the complete sign. In 1951 'Puss' was off on his travels again, this time being returned by the RAF Police from Stockton-on-Tees. In 1953 the cat vanished for the last time – and has not been seen since.

The Parish Council had no option but to have a new cat made and the substitute was installed on its barrel in October, 1953. However, it proved to be no less of an attraction than its predecessor and once again 'Puss' went off on his travels never to return. At this point Mr Walter Klinge enters the story. He was a citizen of Denmark who, at the end of the war, joined Bush Builders of Mile Cross Lane and whilst with them helped to renovate the old house in Spixworth Road known as Greyfriars. The coach house and stable block of this property was turned into a desirable residence, Hunters Lodge, and Mr Klinge was living here when the new cat went missing. He very kindly offered to supply a replacement and in September, 1954, this was ceremonially placed in position atop the sign on the village green.

In November, 1954, a letter from the CO of Horsham St Faiths hinted that the previous cat was now adorning a street sign in Chicago and the parish clerk was instructed to write to the Mayor of Chicago to broach the subject of its return. In due time a reply came thanking the village for its hospitality to US airmen during the war but making no mention of the cat. The Council decided to pursue the subject no further.

Then, in April, 1955, both cat and barrel disappeared. The barrel was later found in the garden of the Vicarage but there was no trace of the 'Puss'. There was some suggestion that he had made his way to the Orkneys or Shetlands and as no Parish Councillor was prepared to spend his precious annual holiday scouring those islands no further action was taken. But Walter Klinge, who by this time had returned to his native Denmark, heard of the loss and immediately offered a replacement. This one, carved in Danish teak, arrived in Old Catton by boat and Royal Mail in January, 1956, and was unveiled at another brief ceremony in July of that year. It has remained in its rightful place ever since, although, on the 12th June, 1971, two men were apprehended trying to remove it (damaging the barrel so much that it had to be replaced) and in June, 1976, the whole sign was toppled over by vandals and was not reinstated until the 13th November, 1976, when it was unveiled by Parish Council Chairman, Mr Bill Catton, at a brief ceremony.

The sign itself, however, had not remained static over the years. Its original home was the village green which, by the 1950s, had become a sort of traffic island and in 1972 was removed completely in order to ease the movement of vehicles. So the sign had to be re-located. It was originally planned for it to be alongside the new school extension in Church Street, but the new development that led to the creation of Parkside Drive quite fortuitously provided a grassy site at its junction with Church Street. And there the cat sits gazing contentedly at St Margaret's Church.

THE VILLAGE YEARS 1900 - 1914

Our original intention was to trace the development of the village, the provision of services and the growth and changes in population through the 20th Century, from 1900 to 2000. But a Census year is such a good statistical starting point that we have plunged in at 1891. In this year Catton was larger and more prosperous than its immediate neighbours, mainly because of the number of 'gentry' residing in large houses in spacious well-appointed grounds. Most of the working class families in the village lived in cottages 'tied' to these mini-estates or, in other cases, 'tied' to the farms surrounding the village. On the surface, it is surprising how few of the families listed in the 1891 Census were still represented in the village in the 1920s, compared with how many of those on the electoral rolls of the 1960s are still here today. However, given that occupants of tied cottages had to move out whenever their employment was, for any reason, terminated, it is more easily understood why the population of those days was continually changing.

In 1891 the focal point of the village was, unmistakably, Catton Hall, perched on the highest point with clear but distant views of Norwich and the Cathedral, and having just celebrated its centenary. Living there was Samuel Gurney Buxton with his wife, Mary Anne (née Birkbeck), nine children and eleven resident staff. The cottages in Church Street, with the exception of the two adjoining Beechwood at the Spixworth Road junction, and all the cottages in Spixworth Road between Church Street and The Maids Head were occupied by the Catton Hall domestic servants and estate workers. The total number of employees, including the blacksmith, saddler, farm steward, gamekeeper, butler, seamstress and nursery nurse, exceeded forty.

Nearby, at the top end of Church Street, was The Manor House, acknowledged as the oldest house in Catton and probably dating from the middle of the Fifteenth Century. Colonel Algernon Dawson, JP, was soon to live there and indeed continued to do so until he retired to Lowestoft in 1930. He was a good friend of the Buxton family and readily joined in the varied social occasions at the Hall and it was he who enlarged The Manor House on the northern side as the century began – the extension was designed to blend in with the old house but the difference in timber work can be clearly seen.

The house known as Catton Court on St Faiths Road was owned by Mr Bullard of the Norwich Brewery and several tied cottages were nearby, whilst next door (if that is properly descriptive of two neighbouring houses each of them in their own large grounds) was The White House then owned by Mr Donald Steward, another brewer. Still further along St Faiths Road was yet another member of the alcohol fraternity. He was Mr Thomas Carter, wine merchant, who lived with his Swiss wife, Adeline, in The Elms. Just across the road from them, in The Red House, lived Miss Millard who had been the Church Street School Manager.

Along Spixworth Road, the legal members of the gentry seem to have congregated. Colonel Berkely-Mansel, JP, lived in Catton House, Mr Overbury, solicitor, lived in The Firs and Mr Rackham, solicitor, in The Cottage. In Eastwood and Beechwood lived retired army officers.

All of these well-appointed houses had tied cottages or lodges for their domestic staff (in addition to the live-in servants), providing accommodation and employment for most of the village's working class. Other tied cottages were associated with the farms that abutted Catton on its western and northern edges – there were three of them next to Norman's Farm in St Faiths Road and a further six towards the top end of that road. Two more were at the rear of Catton Old Hall in Lodge Lane, which itself, at this time, was a rather run down farm house occupied by the farmer, Mr Tallowin. These cottages shared, more often than not, an outside tap or well and outside lavatories or middens and were lit by oil lamp.

There were some privately owned cottages like the one on the corner of Taylors Lane. This was owned by the Bullock family and was an odd building which was added to bit by bit, as occasion demanded; it had a well under the kitchen floor and a pump over the sink to draw the water up. Down in the Catton Grove area, which was then part of the village, was a sprinkling of other cottages, one of them occupied by Mr Charles Betts, a prominent market gardener and another by Mr Pye, the local shepherd. Mr Pye's daughter, Blanche, was a scholar and we shall meet her later as she dedicated her life to teaching at the village school. Behind the Grove Villas, built in 1891, was an area known as Rackham Fields consisting of fifty to sixty rudimentary cottages, some of them, in fact, being little more than shacks. Mr Attoe, the lime merchant, lived in his cottage off St Clements Hill near to his lime pits.

In Church Street, in the cottage adjoining the churchyard, lived Mr Plowman, the saddler. His home had, until recently, formed part of The Magpie public house which had been kept by his father, Robert Plowman, and which was now closed down and converted into two dwellings. It was said that The Magpie had been shut to placate the gentry who considered it too close to the church. There were, however, two other pubs in the Village, The Maids Head and The Woodman, whilst The Royal Oak and The George and Dragon were only just inside the Sprowston parish boundary. It was in the little corner, where George Hill met North Walsham Road, that the only shops were to be found – a butcher, a grocer, together with another blacksmith. The villagers were used to growing their own vegetables, whilst milk and cheese were obtainable from the dairy farm in

Church Street or some of the other farms on the outskirts of the village. Otherwise it was a long walk into Norwich, usually Botolph Street or Magdalen Street, for essentials such as clothing and ironmongery. The only two industrial initiatives were the brickworks on Lodge Lane and the lime burners near Catton Grove – The Grove itself was a well established private lunatic asylum.

In the centre of the village, in Church Street in fact, stood St Margaret's Church unchanging over the centuries but expanded and renovated recently by the Revd Richard Hart and also, a few hundred yards away, the new National School built in 1874 by Mr S G Buxton. Both these establishments spread their authority far beyond the confines of the today's village, for at the beginning of the century Catton extended along Constitution Hill and Angel Road and halfway to Cromer Road. The school regularly taught pupils from Philadelphia Lane in one direction and Spixworth in the other – a daunting walk for four-year olds!

This then was Catton at the end of the Nineteenth Century and generally speaking the ensuing period was one of stability and confidence in the country. A feeling of national pride had been aroused by the Boer War which after the initial reverses of 'Black Week' saw British arms triumph. Moreover, the public at home could see evidence of this by the marvel of the new cinematograph and also felt more closely involved by the volunteer battalions who had trooped off to the Veldt. For Catton itself, in 1900, the trams arrived! Not actually in the village but at least in Denmark Road so that shopping trips could be extended to city centre emporiums such as Chamberlins and Curls. The villagers still had to walk down St Clements Hill, although some were now using bicycles which were, perhaps, in their golden age.

Catton was slowly expanding. In 1898 four cottages were built in Taylors Lane, two of them tied to The Manor House and two to The White House, the two outside ones having extra large gardens for the respective gardeners and the inner two allocated to the respective coachmen. These were shortly followed by the terrace of houses in Lodge Lane, built for the brick-workers, and by a longer terrace in Spixworth Road erected on the instructions of Donald Steward of The White House, just before he died in 1898, expressly for his brewery workers at Steward and Patteson of Pockthorpe. All of these were built with the distinctive red bricks of the Lodge Lane works and, moreover, those in Taylors Lane were equipped with one interior cold tap each!

The roads themselves that serviced the slowly growing community remained largely unchanged during this period. Spixworth Road was the main link with Norwich and a through route to the countryside beyond, as was the North Walsham Road running off at a tangent and linked to Spixworth Road only by George Hill and White Woman Lane. These highways are much the same today but, of course, none of the radial roads from Norwich at that time were bisected by the Ring Road. St Faiths Road, as its name implies, was the main link between Horsham St Faith and Catton and was well used by the farms along that route and it remained so until truncated by the new airfield in 1939. Surprisingly, it was not a main link with Norwich because, after its junction with Fifers Lane, it dwindled into a green track between the conifer plantations of the Buxton estate. It was, however, well used by foot and bicycle as a means of reaching Catton Grove and Mile Cross Lane and was known as 'The Back Road'.

By the side of the roads were several drainage ponds collecting dirty water from the highway – and they *were* dirty at that time with horses plying back and forth all day long! There was one of these ponds at the foot of George Hill, two close to the school, one at each end of Church Street, one further along St Faiths Road and one in Lodge Lane. The one at the top of Church Street, actually on St Faiths Road, was let to a farmer to wash his animals, and the Parish Council was frequently called upon to have it and others sprayed "to prevent the children catching mosquito plague".

Employment during these years continued in the orderly pattern of 1891, domestic service or estate work in connection with the large houses, farm labouring on the land to the west and north, horticultural work on the growing number of market gardens. Nationally the farming industry in the early years of the century was somewhat depressed by the flood of cheap foodstuffs from the Americas and Australasia but it is difficult to find evidence of that in Catton. Certainly the market gardens were profiting from the growing affluence of the industrial towns and cities. Norwich was an obvious market and, in addition, the new railways made it practicable to send fresh fruit and vegetables much further afield, particularly Covent Garden. The light, sandy soils in the village, especially the land between Spixworth Road and North Walsham Road, were well suited for this purpose and had long been recognised as such. George Lindley, that well known 18th Century nurseryman, had a smallholding here. Glasshouses with their attendant boiler houses dotted the area. Mr C O Betts was growing copious quantities of cucumbers and tomatoes under glass for the Covent Garden trade. The large farms growing the more conventional crops were established on the west and north and George Gowing of Lower Hellesdon was the most influential here.

Then there were the self-employed tradesmen (who were often estate workers as well) scattered throughout the village. The Badcock family operated a well established wheelwrights and blacksmiths forge in Church Street (the gates at the entrance to the Village Hall are the work of William Badcock in 1876). Nearby, Herbert Plowman, the saddler and harness maker, was slowly going blind from the intensity of his work. Ted Barnes was the wheelwright in School Lane and, close by, Mark Orsborn not only kept The Woodman public house but was also a bricklayer (his son later became the village undertaker); Henry Harrowven was a wheelwright and blacksmith and also looked after the Post Office.

Whilst the ordinary people of the village worked locally, paradoxically the gentry, for the most part, worked in the city and could be seen every morning making their way to their offices. As time went on the gigs, pony and traps and coaches used for this commuting gradually gave way to the motor car and an entirely new category of employment appeared in Catton – that of chauffeur.

No doubt a jaunt in a new-fangled chauffeur driven motor car was considered a very acceptable diversion. But in any case the gentry were not lacking in forms of entertainment. There were well tended gardens for walking in. These could be formal or informal, orchards, lawns or kitchen gardens. Catton Hall had three ornamental ponds to catch the eye, one with a clam shell fountain centre piece (the one now cared for by the Old Catton Society), one combined with a rockery in the rose garden and a third one (rounded and tiled) on the edge of the Victorian planted conifer wood. Most of the large houses had their own tennis courts and bowling greens, cricket was played in the grounds of Catton Hall – but only after the hay crop had been harvested – and Catton Hall could also boast of a Racquets Court and a paved and edged area in front of the Orangery Museum which, in winter, was flooded and subsequently skated on. The Museum itself was an interesting divertissement being filled with stuffed animals and birds, trophies of foreign holidays and a reminder of John Henry Gurney's reputation as an ornithologist. The school children were happy enough to skate on the frozen pond by the side of the school or sledge down the slopes of Reeve's Meadow and, in seasonal rotation, they would play with hoops, tops, marbles, skipping ropes or went tiddling, flower picking or perhaps apple scrumping. Their parents would play cards or visited the pubs, several of which had pleasure gardens open in the summer. There were also occasional organised entertainments in the Museum for the villagers, such as Black and White Minstrel Shows and lantern slide shows of foreign parts; Caroline Buxton was a well known Edwardian traveller.

This placid way of life was not in the least disturbed by a major administrative change that took place in 1907. After five years of negotiation, Parliament finally gave the go-ahead to a considerable expansion of Norwich and on the 9th November, 1907, the southern part of Catton, St Clements Hill, Catton Grove and the like, was absorbed into the city and at a stroke the official population of Catton was halved to just over 600. Both St Margaret's and Church Street School, however, continued to cater for a catchment area far beyond the civil parish boundaries. In the school Blanche Pye was just commencing her life long career of teaching children.

A much greater impact on the people of Old Catton was made in the summer of 1912. The weather had much more influence on life than it does now and the summer of 1912 was one of those awful, unremitting wet ones. It rained and rained; 11¼ inches over the month of August, including 7½ inches on the 26th

August. This was not just inconvenient, it was disastrous. There were no corn dryers available for the farmers, stooks stood in the fields to dry out and grain crops were more vulnerable to storm damage and mildews. The one consolation was that the village was high enough to escape the floods that swept through Norwich. The nearest the waters of the River Wensum got to Old Catton was the top end of Magdalen Street and one tale that went round the village was that the blacksmith's son, Jack Badcock, had boated all the way up Magdalen Street as far as The Artichoke in order to get home. Further out in the County, the roads from Old Catton to Aylsham and North Walsham were cut when the bridges at Hevingham and Horstead were both washed away.

The following year there was another, but entirely different type of event to excite the village. B C Hucks, a notable pioneer aviator, landed on a prepared field at The Tills on Sunday, 23rd March, 1913, for a week long programme of flying displays. Midweek he announced that any person wishing to fly with him could do so, provided they were under 11 stone and could pay the fee of £5. Eight daring citizens took up the offer but they had to be flown off from Mousehold as the Catton field was deemed not adequate for passenger flights.

But the most sensational occurrence took place on the night of October 29th, 1908. It was then that Police Sergeant Slater patrolling up the road towards Spixworth discovered the body of a young woman huddled in the grass verge close to the outskirts of the village. She was, or had been, Eleanor (Nellie) Howard and she had been stabbed by her lover Horace Larter who gave himself up two days later at Norwich Police Station. The inquest was held at The Maids Head, not more than a mile from the scene of the crime, and Horace Larter's guilt was confirmed. Neither of the leading characters in this drama lived in Catton – she lived with her grandfather in Hainford and he lived with his parents in Ber Street – but the event was symbolic perhaps of how outside forces were soon to intrude with death and bloodshed into the village way of life.

THE GREAT WAR 1914 - 1918

War did not come as a complete surprise on the 4th August, 1914. It had been in the air for some time but there was a certain amount of excitement when our ultimatum to Germany expired. Britannia Barracks was just one of scores of regimental depots busily accepting reservists back into the army and by the end of the month Kitchener's famous poster was everywhere seeking volunteers for his 'New Army'.

In Old Catton, however, as elsewhere in the County, the urgency of all this was secondary to the need for getting in the harvest and the usual tasks continued uninterrupted. So in the early days life in the village went on very much as before and it was only in the Autumn that farm workers began drifting off to the recruiting offices. When it was realised that the war would not "be over by Christmas" and the heavy losses at Gallipoli and Loos filtered through, more and more men left. The women of Catton were also tempted to move as the need for shells and other armaments became clear and it was realised that to work in a factory was not only patriotic but financially rewarding.

Army units were constantly coming and going along the roads of Norfolk, as they were switched from coastal defence to the embarkation ports, and they were periodically billeted in Catton; one villager remembers a Black Watch battalion being billeted in the North Walsham Road area, with a canteen for them set up in a shed alongside the White House in George Hill and their mules being stabled in School Lane. This could possibly be a post-war memory. Villagers might just have seen the Zeppelin, L4, in the early hours of the 20th January, 1915, as it returned from the first Zeppelin raid of the war bombing Sheringham, Hunstanton and Kings Lynn. From April, 1916, onwards they might have seen newly manufactured planes flying from Mann Egerton's factory in Cromer Road to the airfield on Mousehold where they were given a final check-over before delivery to the RFC. Just a year or two previously this airfield had been the Cavalry Drill Ground – a clear pointer to the future of war.

The first tangible effect of the war on Catton was the opening of Catton Hospital on the 2nd of September, 1915. It was one of 62 such auxiliary hospitals that were founded in Norfolk to supplement the giant Military Hospital at Thorpe St Andrew where 45,000 men were treated during the war. The wounded came into Thorpe Station in long ambulance trains, were taken to Thorpe St Andrew for treatment and then were transported to the auxiliary hospitals for convalescence. There were 28 beds at Catton and during the war a total of 687 patients were cared for, so that the soldiers, in their blue uniforms with white shirts and red ties, became a familiar sight in the village. The beds were in the Racquets Court of Catton Hall, and the Museum, with a covered verandah along its front and a lean-to kitchen specially built on one side, was used as the day room. There were also 3 wooden huts on the rink which were for the use of soldiers who had been gassed and for whom constant fresh air was essential. Mrs Laura Buxton took charge of the general administration of the hospital and ran it with great efficiency (she was, after all, a member of the Gurney family) but the only trained medical staff were a nurse and a masseuse. There was, however, no lack of voluntary helpers from the village, additional food was supplied by the Catton Hall kitchens and Mr Buxton, himself, brought back regular supplies of tobacco and cigarettes from the city in his pony and trap; he also supplied, twice a week, a pint of beer for each patient allowed to drink. The pony and trap additionally was pressed into use to pull a string of Bath chairs around the grounds of the Hall so that those unable to walk could enjoy the scenery and fresh air.

The more active of the men often ambled around the village chatting to all and sundry but especially, of course, the girls! Keeping these wounded soldiers entertained was the main pre-occupation of the voluntary helpers and there were frequent concert parties and outings. Handicrafts were encouraged and organised and one of the most popular of these was embroidery. Blanche Pye, then in her thirties, was a regular helper at the hospital, so no doubt her skill with the needle was passed on to many a willing convalescent and, in return, she found no lack of volunteers to inscribe a poem or jingle in her autograph book. This book still survives, in the proud possession of her nephew.

The established way of life in the village was being more and more eroded by the war. In Norwich a general blackout was ordered on the 20th September, 1915, and women increasingly took the place of men, in factories and offices, delivering the post, driving trams. At the school in Church Street, Miss Woolnough was absent for several days in October, 1915, mourning the death of her father in Flanders, whilst on the 4th July, 1917, the School Log records that very few children arrived for school because the "air raid alarm horn" had sounded earlier. The Womens' Land Army was formed to help on the farms which were suffering not only from a shortage of men but also from a severe shortage of horses as they were continually impressed into the army to compensate for the enormous wastage in Flanders. As a result of the U-Boat campaign there were severe food shortages and to make matters worse, a flu epidemic broke out in the Autumn of 1918.

Overseas the war ground on and men from Catton were playing their part. One such was Second Lieutenant D G Buxton, lately of Catton Hall but now of the King's Royal Rifle Corps; his battalion was part of the 2nd Division which had been on stand-by for the Italian Front but which was then switched to reinforce the defenders of the salient formed by the successful British tank attack at Cambrai in November 1917. Lt Buxton survived the fierce German counter-attacks but one of his men, Corporal Richardson, had his hand partly blown off and eventually came back to Old Catton with his officer to take up work on the Buxton Estate as a gardener. One of those who did not return was Lieutenant Ivo Gascoigne of the Grenadier Guards, the only son of Captain and Mrs Gascoigne of The Warren on Spixworth Road. He had been educated at Harrow and Sandhurst, but this was brought to nought by a sniper's bullet on the 12th April, 1918, and his name is on the Old Catton War memorial along with sixteen other Old Catton men. Mostly they died in Flanders but one, Private Thomas Bunting, is recorded as having been killed in Salonika in October, 1918, and another, Corporal Jacob Hurn, died of wounds in Italy in December, 1918. Thomas Bunting had lived in Church Street with his family and had been a gardener on the Catton Hall estate – his son, John, also eventually worked there as a gardener. Leonard Goldspink was another estate worker whose name is on the memorial, and another name is Leonard Graves who was the son of a former Chairman of the Parish Council.

Finally, the war had ended – or at least there was an armistice and the fighting had stopped. Demobilisation commenced and priority was given to farm workers (along with miners and transport workers) so that Old Catton was one of the first places to welcome back its men. One of these was Conway Bullock whose only time away from the village was during his service in the army, and when he returned he came with a medal for gallantry. And for those who did not come back poignant memorials appeared all over the British Isles. The Old Catton Memorial was erected in 1921 on land donated by Mr Edward Buxton (on the edge of the Deer Park). It was sponsored by public subscription and was dedicated on the 3rd of April, 1921, in a quiet but impressive ceremony by the Vicar, the Revd Bernard Mahon, after leading a procession of the choir, British Legion members and others from St Margaret's Church.

1. The unveiling of the Coronation Village Sign at the junction of Church Street with St Faiths Road in June, 1937.

2. The Church Street cottages here seen standing behind the sign of the former Magpie Inn. This picture shows that the present wrought iron railings were not the original enclosure for these cottages.

3. The scene of Nellie Howard's murder in 1908 as shown in a contemporary post card *(from collection of Richard Barham)*.

4. A post card shows an interested crowd gathered outside The Maids Head, where the murder inquest took place *(from collection of Richard Barham)*.

5. Catton Voluntary Aid Hospital - the day room inside Catton Hall museum (now the Village Hall) *(Courtesy A Buxton).*

7. Mrs Barton (hospital quartermaster), Laura Buxton, Corporal Southgate, and Privates Kemper, Patterson, Mitchell, Turner and Riches, seen in the yard beside the hospital day room *(Courtesy A Buxton).*

6. The War Memorial as
originally erected at
Spixworth Road in 1921.
The column and cross
were removed in 1970.

8. Old Catton Baker John Lane photographed on North Walsham Road *(J Lane)*.

9. The Woodman Crossroads: the cottages behind the milk cart stand on what is now The Woodman car park, with the gabled smithy beyond.

11. The Woodman Crossroads in the 1930s, after the installation of traffic lights and widening of the junction.

10. The first Old Catton Post Office at North Walsham Road (probably 1914) with postmistress Mrs Harrowven.

12. Alice Osborn stands in front of her Post Office at North Walsham Road, to the north of The Woodman, in 1944 *(Courtesy The Woodman).*

GROWING UP 1918 - 1939

These were years of urban and suburban spread. Norwich was spreading out into the green fields, in particular building large council house estates, such as Eaton, Earlham and Mile Cross. Catton Grove and Angel Road, now part of the city suburb of New Catton, were similarly built up. Villages on the northern fringes rapidly filled and expanded but Old Catton had little available land. The gentry still lived in their large houses with their expansive gardens, Catton Hall Park was serenely untouchable and the farms on the edge of the village were still fully cultivated. Nevertheless sporadic and piece-meal building took place in Old Catton and, in the main, comprised modern well built houses (such as the sturdy ones in Grange Close) with gas, electricity and indoor toilets, albeit still draining into garden cesspits. This led to an influx of 'upwardly mobile' families willing to commute into Norwich.

In 1927/8 a row of terrace council houses was built in White Woman Lane, actually in Spixworth but intended for Old Catton families, and well away from the village centre – as was the habit in those days. These had no inside water and no modern sanitation. Later on, in 1937/8, more were built in Longe Road and again these did not have modern sanitation, each block of four being allocated a single outside tap with inside drainage consisting of a bucket under the sink! What they did have, perhaps, was their own ghost! As the name of the Lane implies, there was the ghost of a young woman dressed in white roaming the vicinity – whether she once lived in Spixworth Hall and committed suicide on hearing of her lover's death in the King's service or whether she was a Catton girl who married unhappily at Sprowston Church is a matter of preference. Frank Betts vividly remembers seeing the figure of a white lady when walking his dog along the Lane (then just a narrow track), her arms were outstretched and her head turned to one side. It was the middle of a winter's afternoon and Frank was just ten years old and had never heard of any ghost story. Contrarily, Walter Holmes and his sister were cycling along White Woman Lane to their Sprowston home after an evening country dancing at The Cross Keys at Horsham St Faith when they both saw in front of them two figures in long black coats and black hats. As they braked hard so the figures disappeared.

FARMING

These were not, however, halcyon days. Despite a time of euphoria immediately following the war, the period was largely one of hardship resulting from world-wide trading upsets. Wages in Britain started to be reduced and the miners' strike over this led to the nine days General Strike. Of more immediate effect to Old Catton was the reduction of farm wages in 1921, from 45 shillings per week to 25 shillings per week, and a brief strike of farm workers failed to alter this, although in March, 1929, a minimum wage of 30 shillings per week was introduced.

The farms in the neighbourhood of Old Catton still carried on producing their traditional crops of barley, wheat and oats. The innovative crop of sugar beet was only just starting to show up in the fields of Norfolk and the Cantley sugar factory, although built in 1912, was only now, in 1920, switching to continuous operation. *Mr Frank Shorten:* "I remember watching, in 1928, a sugar beet topping and lifting demonstration by machine at the bottom end of Taylors Lane".

Farm work still relied heavily on the horse and particularly so on the arable fields of Catton. Horses pulled the ploughs, the drills and the harrows. At harvest time the binder was pulled by a three horse team but even so the work was so hard that the horses were changed every three hours. In addition, all carting needed the horse for motive power and this applied not only to the conventional short range farming movements but also to carting over greater distances. There was regular carting of spent hops from the Pockthorpe Brewery to be used as manure for the fields and they also brought back from the brewery cinder ash for track mending – Taylors Lane was surfaced in this way. But by 1930 farm tractors were becoming more evident and horses were declining in number (not for nothing was the size of the combustion engine related to horse power!) and traction engines were a common sight as they pulled contractors' farm machinery out of their Norwich depots and onto the farms all around; these were thirsty machines and were often seen filling up with water at the George Hill and St Faiths Road ponds.

Harvest time was the summit of all these activities and at the appropriate time it seemed as if the whole village would go off to the fields. Wives prepared for a long day's work, children for a day of excitement; they were armed with sticks to, hopefully, hit the rats and rabbits as they ran out from the uncut area in the centre of the field, steadily getting smaller and smaller. There would be picnics on the field, as time permitted, and the farmer would provide ample supplies of beer which often came in wicker-encased jugs. The money for this would be found by auctioning the dead rabbits at the end of the day. *Mr Jimmy Boulter:* "My father was team leader with the horses on Frank Gowing's farm and when I was eight I was allowed to sit on the lead horse at harvest time as the 'hold you', taking my cue from the men, two on top of the cart and two loading sheaves from below. Later I worked for the Gowings at Hellesdon Hall Farm for two years and then spent thirty three years at Catton Hall Farm with my wife (who had been a Land Army girl)".

The most important farmer was Frank Gowing who rented and lived at Old Hall Farm in Lodge Lane, and owned most of the land to the west of St Faiths Road and also Norman Farm on the eastern side of St Faiths Road. Horses were stabled at this farm and most of his twenty men and boys lived in the tied cottages nearby so it is not surprising that Taylors Lane was in constant use as they took whatever machinery was needed to the fields – identified by such names as 'Hands', 'Mushroom' and 'Meadow Spot'. *Miss Maire Booty:* "The farm hands used to groom and saddle the horses first thing in the morning and then take them and the ploughs and other equipment down Taylors Lane, sometimes going on up to the Wharton Farm on Bullock Hill". Mr Gowing sold Norman Farm in 1938 to the Pointer family who thereupon turned it into a dairy farm, whilst his fields further along Fifers Lane, together with those of John Wharton, disappeared when the airfield was built. There was also Mr Landamore's Rose Lodge Dairy Farm, extending along both sides of the northern part of St Faiths Road, north of Lodge Lane. In the middle of the village, in Church Street, stood Catton Hall Farm, another dairy farm. *Mr W G Holmes:* "My father was a stockman at Sprowston Hall, looking after Red Poll cattle, but he moved to Catton Hall Farm in 1927 to run the dairy farm and I remember the cows being turned out onto the pasture behind the school. My main job, though, was looking after the horses at the Hall".

MARKET GARDENS

If the farms were the stolid backbone of the agrarian scene, market gardens were their opportunist, quick-witted, almost frivolous companions. They were busy supplying the ever-growing and varying demand of the urban areas and the light soils between Spixworth Road and North Walsham Road were dotted with greenhouses, often with attendant boiler houses and water tanks and the occasional static steam engine to steam clean the soil. The largest and most flourishing market gardeners here were Mr Morgan, Mr Page, and the Betts brothers, and there were large acreages of tomatoes and other salad crops under glass, and rows of soft fruit in the open. There were also more exotic crops, such as asparagus, chrysanthemums and maiden-hair fern, this last being for the florists of Norwich to include in their bouquets. *Mr Frank Betts:* "I was born on the eighteen acre holding run by my father and uncle, at the junction of White Woman Lane and Spixworth Road. We had a wooden bungalow, which at the time was the only building on White Woman Lane. My grandfather had perfected a smooth tomato which sold at Covent Garden for 12 shillings a stone. We grew mainly tomatoes, cucumbers and lettuces and the maiden-hair fern". To the south of the Deer Park (the last deer died out in the winter of 1926) and The Warren were the smallholdings of Mr Carter and Mr Airey. They grew the more mundane vegetables for the local markets and as Mr Airey was also the village night soil contractor, some villagers were reluctant to purchase his produce! Reeves Nurseries, which specialised in growing roses, spread along much of the south side of Lodge Lane, whilst tucked into the north western corner of this road was Frank Hunt's holding, again growing vegetables which he sold from his horse and cart. Just a little further along the Spixworth Road were the mushroom sheds of Geoffrey Hannent.

SHOPPING

Old Catton, unlike Hellesdon and Sprowston, remained very much a village with few facilities. What shops existed were at the very edge of the village (even technically in Sprowston) along the North Walsham Road. At the George Hill crossroads were two long established shops, the grocery business of Bob Clarke, who also doubled up as a chimney sweep, and Tyrrell the newsagent. Mr Tyrrell is well remembered for riding a trade bicycle around the village and for various escapades on his AJS motorcycle which, on one occasion, deposited him in the pond at the bottom of George Hill. One of his daughters gave music lessons. Opposite, in one of the two cottages in front of The Woodman was Mr Webb, the butcher; when the cottages were demolished to widen the junction he re-opened on the remaining corner, not far away from Mr Bertie Lebbell, shoe-maker, with Mr Attoe's second-hand furniture shop just down George Hill. A little way into School Lane was Harry Spanton's fish and chip shop opposite the premises of Mr Pendle who started this period as a wheelwright but gradually metamorphosed into carpenter, coffin maker and undertaker. Not far along the North Walsham Road was the busy bakery which John Lane had bought from Bob Arthurton in 1916 and which, after his death in 1931, was successfully managed by his family until 1944. Further along North Walsham Road was another grocers which was largely run by Mrs Fox whilst her husband carried on a carpentry business; a small co-op opened on the opposite side of the road later on. The Post Office was also on North Walsham Road but it was prone to migration. At first it was sited south of the George Hill junction, then it moved to a tin lean-to adjoining the terraces just north of The Woodman and it eventually came to rest in the terraces opposite Dixons Fold. Finally, and as a sign of the times, a petrol station was opened by Mr Day on his demobilisation from the army at the end of the war – his only asset being one surplus army lorry. This later became Duffield's Garage and remained awkwardly situated near the George Hill junction until well after World War II.

In many cases though, instead of the villagers going to the shops, the shops came to the villagers. Cecil Stevens, from School Lane, had a fruit and vegetable round with his pony and cart, whilst rival greengrocers, 'Horry' Carter and Charlie Wrench pushed their heavy two-wheeled barrows around the village laden with fruit. Bob Alpe from Church Farm, Spixworth, and Walter Seaman from Beeston Hall Farm delivered milk from their milk carts, 'Tumbledown Dick' Jermy delivered sweets, groceries and paraffin from his old van (the sweets well flavoured with paraffin). Roys of Coltishall had a bread round to rival that of John Lane, and trade bike deliveries were made by all the other shops. More specialised rounds included the 'Battery Man' from Mile Cross who came with recharged batteries for the wireless and took away the used ones every fortnight, and the 'Ginger Beer Man' from Mile Cross Lane with his stone bottles (he was later replaced by Corona with their purpose-built lorry). Every Autumn the 'Fish Man' cycled up from Caister, complete with hand bell, to sell shrimps.

There was also a sprinkling of village women who were happy to supplement the family income by making and selling sweets, cakes, dresses and the like. Mrs Postle is well remembered for making humbugs on a hook in her whitewashed kitchen in a cottage at the rear of The Old Hall and for selling them at a farthing each, and Jack Badcock's wife in Church Street made fancy pastries for sale.

The shops in Norwich (including the Woolworths in Rampant Horse Street) were also getting closer as the new bus services began to penetrate Old Catton, although, of course, travelling by bus was still a comparative luxury and most continued on foot or by bike. The first contact was made in 1924 by Eastern Motorways whose service to Mundesley stopped at The Woodman en route. A request in 1926 by the Parish Council for buses to run directly into the village was originally refused by this company on the grounds that "buses could not negotiate George Hill" but they relented shortly after and a service was routed down George Hill, along Spixworth Road and on to Buxton. Better remembered was the No 8A service operated by United Auto Services which, in 1927 started a half hourly service to The Woodman and in 1931 extended this to the junction of Church Street and St Faiths Road. This was not very reliable but it was invaluable for city workers and city bound school children. The service was taken over by Eastern Counties in 1931 (trams had ceased operating the previous year) and in 1937 the service was re-numbered 93.

The gentry meanwhile were gradually abandoning horse drawn conveyances in favour of motors. In the immediate post-war years Mr Edward Buxton still went to his office at the bank in a horse drawn gig but sometime in the late twenties he switched to chauffeur-driven cars, a Wolseley and a Sunbeam. At the Manor House Colonel Dawson had in his garage first a Ruston Hornsby and then an Armstrong-Siddeley but nevertheless he was often seen riding around the village on an upright bicycle (and would always doff his hat when passing the War Memorial). Neville Howlett sported a Humber, Mr Finch of The Red House favoured an Austin 16. All were driven by chauffeurs in smart uniforms with peaked caps (although Mr Finch often preferred to drive himself) and Jack Bossom and Mr Bunnett are still remembered amongst their number. When Mrs Crampton moved into The Manor House in 1930 she engaged Arthur Shorten as her chauffeur. For those slightly further down the social scale, motor cycles, with or without sidecars, were an attainable option and there were a goodly number of these to be seen on the roads around Old Catton.

One result of this increase in motor traffic was an upsurge in traffic accidents. At George Hill, a notorious black spot, villagers remember a lorry crashing into The Woodman and, not long after, a motor cycle careering straight through the window of Tyrrell's shop. The ladies tended to remain content with their carriages and Mrs Steward, of The White House, was often seen in hers with Mr Rolfe at the rein. One exception was Mrs 'Bunny' Carrick who rode a motor cycle, then graduated to an Austin Seven and eventually became Eastern Counties first woman bus driver.

LEISURE TIME

For the children of the village summertime was the best time of the year. Quite apart from the School Sports Days and nature lessons held out doors, there were the long summer holidays when the lanes and fields beckoned for adventure. *Miss Maire Booty*: "I spent my childhood in Taylors Lane along with my brother, Leslie Bullock next door and Frank Hunt nearby; in fact you could say we virtually owned the Lane. I remember the wild flowers in the hedgerows, sheets of greater stitchwort, as white as snow, in the spring, clusters of purple violets, wild briars in the hedges, daisies and buttercups in the meadow where the mushrooms grew. The field hedges further down were thick with juicy blackberries in the autumn and there was a prolific crab-apple tree in the bottom field. The gardens of the Red House ended with an orchard which had easily accessible walnut trees. There was a kitchen garden alongside the Red House, where the edge of Catton Chase now stands, and between that and Crome House were Crome House's extensive orchards, impenetrable behind a corrugated iron fence with barbed wire along the top. The cottage of The White House's gardener stood at the corner of what is now Woodland Drive and a small gate there led into a field and, if you could negotiate that without being seen, you could get into the fir tree plantation alongside Woolsey's paddock and from there to the Buxton Woods – much more extensive than they are now at the back of the Recreation Ground – and so to friends' cottages on Spixworth Road. All without being seen!"

A summer event of a different kind was described in the August, 1932, edition of the parish magazine by Mr English, headmaster of the Church Street school, as follows:-

"Those boys who turned out for a cycle run on August 11th, rode very well indeed. Visiting first the old stocks at Haveringland, we next made our way to the Duel Stone at Cawston Woodrow. From there it was a delightful ride to Holt, including the toil up Edgefield Heath Hill. A visit was paid to Captain Marryat's grave in Langham Churchyard and then we went to Morston where we ate our lunches and saw yacht racing on the Blakeney Harbour at the same time. The coast road was then taken to Sheringham and then inland (when the guide went wrong!) via

Blickling Hall and Aylsham. After a short rest and refreshments the last part of the journey was taken home. May this be the first of other similar rides. Arrangements are being made for a party of girls to cycle over to Blickling Hall Gardens on September 1st".

Bill English was well known as a keen cyclist – his enthusiasm must have been catching!

Winter-time was much more sombre; dark and wet evenings with, perhaps, the aroma of toast hanging in the air. Between the school and the smithy was a large pond which, when frozen over, gave ample opportunities for ice-sliding – but not before Mr English had tested its safety with a few well-aimed bricks! There was no Christmas party at the school but the Sunday School was always taken to the Pantomime in January and this invariably included an ice-cream. There were, of course, private Christmas parties, when the girls dressed up in their party frocks in spite of the general lack of heating in the homes. *Mrs Sheila Currall*: "At these parties the Christmas trees were 'undressed' and the sweets and chocolate novelties were distributed amongst the guests; it was very good training as we were not allowed to grab what we liked and it was not easy to see a favourite chocolate animal going home in someone else's pocket".

For the grown-ups most of the entertainment in the village was 'home-made'. There was no TV and the wireless was still in its infancy; in 1922 there was the novelty of cat's-whisker reception and a limited range of programmes but by the late 1930s reception had improved and there was a better choice of programmes (Monday Night at 7, Henry Hall, Saturday Night Theatre). However, in the light bright evenings of summer in Old Catton, sport was the focus of attention. The cricket team played on the pitch at the front of Catton Hall where the Oak tree did duty as the score board and also the team assembly point and tea room. Most of the large houses had their own bowling greens and matches would be played on all of them, to the financial benefit of village boys. *Mr Jimmy Hall*: "We used to earn money by wiping the bowls for the players, some were better tippers than others but it was possible to get as much as a shilling a night. The equipment was stored in the potting shed in the Parish Hall drive and additional tips could be obtained for moving this to and from the greens". The Tennis Club played on the grass court at the rear of the White House in St Faiths Road and an Angling Club met regularly at The Woodman. The licensee of The Woodman at this time was Mr Charles Wicks who, under the stage name of Trumpet Major Wix was a well known entertainer whose specialty was playing the post horn (he was reputed to be able to play two at once!). *Mr Duggie Day*: "I often heard Trumpet Major Wix practising his pieces on The Woodman bowling green very early in the morning. He used to play on stage at the Norwich Hippodrome and often went further afield to such events as the Olympia Horse Shows in London".

From 1919 onwards, the newly acquired Parish Hall was put to regular use by the Women's Institute, the Debating Society (organised by Mr English when he came to the village in 1928), the Horticultural Club and the British Legion, as well as being the venue for whist drives and for sundry dances and concerts. These concerts, as might be guessed, used local talent, such as the ubiquitous Mr English who had a reputation for monologues and humorous songs, Mr Eke (a teacher from the Angel Road School) who drew sketches on the blackboard, Mrs Earl who played the piano, Mrs Woolsey whose specialty was the singing of 'Cherry Ripe' and the two Miss Kings (hairdressers from Sprowston) who performed Scottish dances. A good time was had by all!

THE LODGE LANE BRICKWORKS

This was the only industrial enterprise in Old Catton. It had been started by George Wrench in the 1880s and there were several other similar works in the School Lane area of Sprowston, each of them sitting upon a pocket of Boulder Clay or Brick Earth. By the 1930s Mr Wrench had sold his concern to Robert Ruymp and about a dozen men and boys were employed there, including George Wrench's son who delivered the bricks by horse and cart. Some of the brick-makers lived on the site in a scattering of wooden cottages.

The tall solitary square chimney, protruding from the Hoffman continuously burning kiln, dominated the scene, whilst in the open yard the brick-makers stood at sand covered benches protected from bad weather only by canvas awnings. They were spared the bitter blasts of winter, however, as the danger of frost damage to the soft bricks was too great and the brick-makers were paid off for the season; their only source of income then being periodic digging out more of the clay from the pits. Disused pits made good play areas for the children and the warm flat top of the kiln was a comfortable gathering place. The fine Norfolk Red bricks that were made here were used widely in the village and the four cottages in Taylors Lane, the Red House in St Faiths Road and Mrs Earl's house at 237 Spixworth Road still remain as examples. In the city, the Lads' Club in King Street is an example and we could have cited Norwich Brewery and Ruymp's offices as examples but, alas, they have been redeveloped! *Mr Dennis Woods*: "My father was foreman of the brickworks and we lived in the cottage adjacent to it on Lodge Lane. All the bricks were hand made and the clay from the pug mill was channelled into the making bays where the makers would fill and level the moulds; the wet bricks were then laid out to dry before firing".

Of the local builders who may have made good use of these bricks, the best known was Mr Orsborn of Rose Cottage on North Walsham Road, but there were also Mr Louis Sabberton, who built Louis Close, Mr Lubbock, who built the bungalows on Lodge Lane opposite the brickworks, and Mr John Watts.

WAR AGAIN   1938 - 1945

Well, yes, the war actually started in 1939. But with the overrunning of Austria and Czechoslovakia, there was a trembling of war in the air in 1938. In May of that year Norwich appointed an Air Raid Precautions officer and volunteers were called upon to set up First Aid and Air Raid Posts (talk of decontamination squads was especially daunting). Trenches were dug in Chapel Field Gardens – although they were not actually concreted-in until February of 1939. In Old Catton war came a little closer in 1938 when the Air Ministry, having determined the suitability of the land, began compulsorily purchasing all the fields to the west of St Faiths Road, including Mr Wharton's farmhouse and buildings, for a new airfield.

In other respects, however, 1938 was a good year in Old Catton, as it was in the rest of England. Jobs were becoming more plentiful, partly because of the re-armament programme but especially because of the vitality of new industries such as motor cars and radios, and the motor car was one of the reasons for the new feeling of well being. By 1939 there were two million on the roads, giving freedom of movement and easy access to the countryside. Annual holidays were becoming more customary (the first Butlins opened in 1937). The wireless was in millions of homes, giving undreamt of entertainment as well as instant news of the world at large. Shops gave a greater service than ever before and at bargain prices (Fifty Shilling Tailors!) and cinemas, with a change of programme every week, were hard to resist. Moreover, now that they had a reliable bus service, it was much easier for the Old Catton villagers to reach these facilities in the heart of Norwich.

But the shadow of war was creeping closer to Old Catton, almost literally, as the new airfield began to take shape. Officers Mess, Control Tower, five hangars and a bomb store were built, mostly in red brick (but no concrete runways as the designated bombers were light enough not to need them). The children of Taylors Lane watched it all as they continued to cut across the meadow to Fifers Lane on their various enterprises. They also witnessed the tireless Mr English journeying around the village issuing gas masks and identity cards. In March, 1939, Prime Minister Chamberlain gave Poland a clear guarantee of support in the event of attack. On the 1st September, 1939, the mass evacuation of London began and over the next four days 16,000 children arrived in Norfolk, some of them to find their way to Old Catton. An earlier voluntary survey had identified those houses with spare accommodation and these now filled with apprehensive school children. In the event, though, they mostly did not stay long as the peaceful nature of the 'phoney war' and the strangeness of the quiet rural life encouraged them to return to their homes. That is with the exception of little Rosie Nightingale and her brother Teddy (from Leytonstone) who stayed with the Shorten family throughout the war, attended the Church Street school and to all intents and purposes became Old Catton children, returning to London only after the war.

Quite apart from the sudden increase in population there were other very visible changes to Old Catton in that first September of the war. Windows were criss-crossed with tape and at night were covered with blackout curtains, or shutters, that obliterated all homely light. Social events were thrown into chaos by the immediate closure of the Parish Hall, although people were probably reluctant to leave the security of their homes, and everybody carried a gas mask in its own square cardboard box (they could be fined if they did not!). Car owners were particularly hard hit as not only was petrol the first commodity to be rationed (and stringently) but car headlights had to be heavily masked. Overnight, as it seemed, the new red brick buildings of the airfield were daubed with camouflage paints and within weeks Blenheim bombers flew in amongst the contractors' machinery as they were dispersed from their home base at Watton.

Another more gradual change in the landscape was the emptying of all the large houses in the village during the first year of the war. Captain Buxton left Catton Hall to take command of the 6th Battalion, Royal Norfolks and his family subsequently moved out as the army commandeered the Hall around them. The Carter sisters moved out of The Elms shortly after. The Gough family left Crome House, the Morses vacated The Warren; Greyfriars was speedily requisitioned to become the area ARP headquarters, and local school children happily busied themselves in filling sandbags to protect it, whilst The Warren, The Elms, The White House, Catton House and Eastwood were all, in their turn, commandeered by the army (although it is believed that Lady Mansel and Mr Howlett continued to live in their respective properties).

However, the expected deluge of bombs did not materialise and the main flurries of warlike activity were restricted to the airfield where flights of Spitfires came and went, on detachment from Duxford. Excursions to the seaside were still possible and it was whilst returning from an Easter Monday bus trip to Cromer with her boy friend that a young school teacher, Angela Field, walked past a crashed aeroplane ensnared in the hedge in Fifers Lane and guarded by a solitary soldier with rifle and fixed bayonet. Mishaps must have been quite common at the airfield for only six days later, on the 31st March, Douglas Bader (then just a Flying Officer) crashed his Spitfire (K9858) into a low wall there whilst taking off with others to protect an East coast convoy.

Then the war exploded. On April 9th, Hitler sent his forces into Norway and Denmark and a month later, on May 10th, he invaded The Netherlands and Belgium. German armour reached the English Channel on May 20th and by June 25th France had surrendered and Britain stood alone. Of even greater concern to the people of Old Catton was the knowledge that the enemy was now only just over 100 miles away in Holland and the whole of Norfolk had become a war zone. A ten-mile wide security zone was established along the coast, so that seaside trips were not an option during that summer, and soldiers built and occupied defensive positions along a series of strategic defence lines, with concrete pill boxes popping up like mushrooms. A spigot mortar mount constructed in woodland on the east side of Catton Park survives to this day. Further to the north a lengthy anti-tank ditch was dug from North Walsham Road, where a steel girder road block was ready to be placed in position, through The Tills, along the edge of the Deer Park to the pond on the corner of Church Street, and across Catton Park to Mile Cross Lane where a pill box anchored it. An unfortunate side effect of this digging was that the clay bottom of the pond was ruptured and a subsequent thunderstorm caused it to collapse so that, thereafter, the corner regularly flooded. Air Raid Sirens were now more than just a novelty: Norwich had its first bombs on the 9th July, and Old Catton quickly followed suit as daylight raiders tried to strike at the airfield. Angela Field kept a diary during this period (the school at which she was teaching had been evacuated from St Leonards to Bedford so it was easier to get home) and a particularly eventful day was August 21st:

"2 air raids early on in the morning. Another siren goes and in a few minutes a plane is heard. Mum yells "Get up". Race into clothes; hear pop, pop, pop of machine guns and thud of bomb exploding over on the St Faiths aerodrome. Rush into cupboard under the stairs and then into Carter's dugout for ¾ hour. All Clear about 12.30. Have dinner and then alarm again. Hear L. shout "they're dropping bombs" and get into cupboard while house shakes and vibrates as 5 bombs drop in Catton Park. Spend afternoon in dugout. No appreciable gunfire or any British activity at anytime seen or heard. Siren goes again. All Clear soon after. Siren again, all clear. Stay up till gone 12. Calm night".

Altogether her diary records 65 alerts during August and it may have been one of those that Maire Booty remembers. "Some of the first bombs to fall were on the air-field. It was one afternoon and my brother heard the plane and pronounced it a 'Jerry' because it wasn't making the right noise. He climbed on the water butt and up the drain pipe onto our shed roof, followed by yours truly, who got as far as the edge of the water butt when the plane released its bombs. We stood watching in awe and luckily they landed in soft ground on the airfield and did no damage". Frequent raids continued into the Autumn and on Sunday afternoon, the 27th October, Jimmy Hall standing on his front doorstep in Spixworth Road, was astonished to see two German bombers flying fast and low towards the coast, leaving behind a plume of smoke over Mousehold.

Not all the raiders made it safely back and an impressive funeral, with full military honours including a large contingent from the RAF at St Faiths, was held at St Margaret's for two German airmen. They were crew-men from a Dornier which a day or two earlier had bombed the airfield at Watton and had then been shot down into the sea off Brancaster by a Spitfire from Lincolnshire; their graves remained in the churchyard until well after the war.

Luckily there do not appear to have been any civilian casualties which is all the more surprising as there seems to have been no particular issue of Anderson Shelters. These were shaped sheets of corrugated iron, issued to householders by the government, which, when dug into the back garden and thickly covered with earth, gave very effective protection to the family. In these early days of the war, the residents of Old Catton relied on the cupboard under the stairs or, in the case of some of those living in Church Street, the stoke-holes of the greenhouses across the road. Home life was changing fast. Ration books had been distributed near the end of 1939 and in January, 1940, sugar, butter and bacon were rationed and housewives and shopkeepers had to contend with coupons. *Jim Booty*: "Once a week I cycled to Catton Grove with my granny's ration book and her orders for meat and grocery rations, and further on to Mr Laddiman's in Angel Road for our supplies; these were delivered by trade cycle". There was the nightly ritual of attending to the blackout curtains and blinds and each night there was the need to listen out for the sirens. One source of comfort was the wireless which gave out a stream of reassuring information, and, for security, the news announcers now prefixed the news with their names – Alvar Liddell, Bruce Belfrage and others – which made it seem that much more friendly.

A section of Catton Park was dug up as part of the drive to produce more food. All signposts were removed in order to confuse an invading enemy and this order included the Village Sign which was taken to a 'safe' site just outside the Officers Mess on the airfield; it remained there for the rest of the war. Fifers Lane was closed to civilian traffic and movement in general in the village was somewhat restricted by sentries and barbed wire – the end of Taylors Lane was closed off in this way and the Youngman family, and others living in the row of terraces next to The Maids Head, had to pass a sentry in order to get to their back doors. He was there because the slopes of Catton Park were now in use as an encampment for various army units as they reformed and built up their numbers after Dunkirk. Another sentry was posted outside The Warren where more troops were billeted, members of the

ATS were housed in The Grange and Catton Hall itself was commandeered as a Headquarters. A solitary barrage balloon flew from the top of Constitution Hill.

The airfield, meanwhile, was now officially designated Horsham St Faiths. It had been formally opened on the 1st June, 1940, and allocated to No 2 Group, RAF, who decided to station Blenheim bombers of N°s. 114 and 139 Squadrons there. These continued to carry the war to the enemy, along with the rest of Britain's meagre bomber force, and were turning more and more to night bombing as some protection from enemy guns. Unfortunately this incurred an increased difficulty of finding the target and finding the way home and, as winter approached, also incurred the considerable hazards of bad weather flying. It was icing that caused a Blenheim to crash onto Norma Roll's house on the corner of Dixons Fold. This was on the night of 27th November, 1940, and it was one of 114 Squadron's planes returning from a raid on Cologne; it had flown out from Oulton airfield and was attempting to land at the better equipped St Faiths airfield because of the bad weather. It crashed into the orchard at the rear of the house and one engine wedged fast against the back door; luckily there was no fire and all three crew members, although injured, were brought safely into the house to await the ambulance. The crew were Canadians and Norma's father was relieved to hear their accents coming from the scene of the crash (including a yell to "Get me out of this bloody plane!") as he had presumed that the plane was German.

The New Year saw Old Catton buckling down to a serious war. The Home Guard were now all uniformed and reasonably armed and daily becoming more proficient. Old Catton members, such as Mr English, Mr Holmes and Mr Fish, formed part of the Spixworth company. *Mr Holmes:* "I was encouraged by Mr English to volunteer for training as a signaller as this was organised at The Warren and therefore nearer home". They were ably supplemented by the older children of the village, not in a martial way but in all sorts of voluntary activities. The Guides, the 1st Old Catton Guide Company, were busy collecting waste paper, jam jars, rose hips (to make syrup) and acorns (to feed to the pigs). Iris Youngman was one of the teenagers who spent an afternoon each week rolling bandages and knitting gloves and balaclavas. Rationing was now a way of life. Meat, margarine and tea had been added to the list of rationed foodstuffs following the fall of France and, in 1941, cheese was added and tinned foods and clothing were rationed by a new 'points coupon' system – which meant that a pair of scissors was an even more necessary accessory on a shop counter. Eggs, on the other hand, came under a 'controlled distribution' – shopkeepers had to share them out as and when they became available.

Then during the second half of 1941 the war took a dramatic change of direction. In June Hitler invaded the USSR and in December Japan attacked the Phillipines and Malaya, and each of these actions had a direct effect on Old Catton. There were no air raids from August, 1941, to April, 1942, because the Luftwaffe was fully committed on the Eastern Front and the 18th Division, including three territorial battalions of the Royal Norfolks, was diverted to Singapore and extinction. Jack Hunt, Leslie Smith and John Lane were just three of the Old Catton men who became prisoners of war of the Japanese and there were others amongst the POWs who also had fond memories of Old Catton. They were the men of 125 Anti-Tank Regiment (actually a Sunderland territorial unit) who had spent a muddy winter and a long summer on Catton Park before leaving for embarkation at Gourock on the 30th October, 1941. They had never fired their guns in anger because the ship carrying them had been sunk just outside Singapore.

There was still no shortage of troops in the village, however, as a battalion of the Gordon Highlanders, complete with pipe band and full ceremonial dress moved in. They made a lasting impression on the children of the village. The bandsmen were billeted at The Elms and almost daily marched down to Catton Hall with the sound of pipes and drums resonating along St Faiths Road. The officers were quartered in The White House and Catton Hall, there were more troops on the Park and the Parish Hall became their NAAFI (after the stuffed animals and birds were removed and stored in the Racquets Court). *Maire Booty*: "I remember them holding a Highland Games in Catton Hall grounds on the same day that we had a Battle of Britain Fete there; the games included tossing the caber, highland dancing and piping competitions. Eventually they left for Beeston St Lawrence for more training before going overseas where, rumour had it, they suffered severe casualties."

Then, rather like a thunderstorm at the end of a fine summer's day, the eight month lull in air raids came to an abrupt and devastating end for Norwich on the night of the 27th/28th April, 1942. It was a 'Baedeker Blitz' (a revenge attack for the RAF bombing of Lubeck) and the thunder was caused by just under 30 Luftwaffe bombers. Most of the damage took place in the general area of Barn Road – possibly because the pathfinder mistook City Station for Thorpe Station. Amongst those rendered homeless was the Carter family of Dereham Road who moved into temporary accommodation in The Avenues until Mrs Carter met, by chance, her former employer, Mrs Jewson of the Old House in Old Catton. When Mrs Jewson heard of the family's misfortune she insisted that they move into the cottage at the rear of the Old House, even to the extent of rehousing her two daughters, May and Doris. A happy sequel was that the Carter's daughter, Eileen, met and married her husband in Old Catton in 1950.

It was certainly safer in Old Catton but the nearness of the airfield made the village vulnerable to near misses. *Barbara Lockwood (née Sexton)*: "When the all-clear went after one late night raid we left our shelter in the field only to find unexploded incendiary bombs dotted about in the grass like silver baseball bats.

Then we noticed smoke and flames coming from The Elms to our right (it was unoccupied at the time). Dad informed the Air Raid Warden and then he and Mr Pointer dashed for the stirrup pumps and next thing, mum, myself and Mrs Pointer found ourselves on the pumps. We didn't put it out but we did stop it spreading and when I had time to look up at the sky it was getting light". This was the same morning that Mrs Wright, living on St Faiths Road, discovered that an incendiary had gone through the guttering of the house and had ignited on the lawn. On another occasion a batch of incendiaries fell on Mr Scarlett's chicken houses on Lodge Lane. Whilst sometime during the summer of 1941 Arthur Cannings, on guard duty at the top of Constitution Hill, had a perfect view of a Junkers 88 making a low level daylight attack on the airfield only for the stick of bombs to fall in the grounds of Eastwood, The Grange and Catton Park. This was much too close for young Daphne Sandle who was cycling along Oak Lane at the time; she was unhurt and quickly recovered when Mrs Watson, of the end cottage opposite The Beeches, took her in for a cup of tea and a sit down.

Mr Cannings was awaiting induction as aircrew and had been temporarily posted to RAF Old Catton which was, in fact, a large collection of huts centred around the underground bunker (still there alongside Chartwell Road) which acted as the meteorological centre for N⁰· 3 Group. On one occasion it also became for a short time the nerve centre for the fighter squadrons at Coltishall when their Control Room was knocked out.

Meanwhile Horsham St Faiths was still at the forefront of RAF actions and on the 31st May, 1942, had the distinction of launching the first bombing mission by the new 'wooden wonder', the Mosquito. This was almost the final fling by the RAF at this base as, in September, the Mosquito Squadrons were moved to Marham and the airfield was handed over to the fast expanding USAAF. They briefly brought in B26 Marauder bombers to continue the light bomber role of the base but they left for North Africa in November. Then, after a short stay by three Thunderbolt fighter squadrons, the airfield closed down completely in July, 1943, which must have been a considerable surprise for the villagers. It had been assigned to heavy bombers of the USAAF and three massive concrete runways had to be built for them.

However, there was still military activity in the village for by now Catton Hall had been taken over as a headquarters for a training unit under the overall control of the 76th Division, which by a happy choice had for its insignia a red Norfolk Wherry on a black ground.

The ATS who worked in the offices there were very happy with their surroundings, the banks of rhododendrons along the length of the drive and the camellias in the conservatory (they were threatened with dire penalties if they went anywhere near them). *Betty Davis*: "One of our offices was in an upstairs room with a large balcony and, in good weather, we used to take our typewriters out onto it and worked away surrounded by all that lovely garden. A wisteria grew all over the balcony wall and I always think of Catton Hall when it is in bloom". She also remembers a friend who longed to slide down the banisters of the hall staircase. One of the officers at this HQ formed a small concert party from amongst the staff which was then taken on tour around units in Norfolk – they called themselves 'The Cat on Hot Bricks'. The difficulty of finding material for costumes (a matter of some importance as the clothes ration had been cut by a quarter in the spring of 1942) was overcome by soaking a load of surplus paper in the bath until it turned into a sort of cloth!

One of the young soldiers posted here for advanced training was private Simkin. He had been called up in 1942, had done his basic training at Catterick, trained as a signaller at Bury and Coventry and then, in February 1943, was posted to Catton Hall. This suited him very well as his home was in Thorpe. The members of his intake were billeted on the top floor of the Hall (sleeping on straw-filled palliases) and they spent their days on drills, inspections and route marches; once a week they marched to the old public baths in St Andrews Street. They were sent to Drayton Hall for tropical kit issue and inoculations and then moved back to Eastwood House until, in the early hours of the 14th April, 1943, they were convoyed to North Walsham station to entrain for Liverpool. By the 23rd April they were disembarking in Algiers.

Just three months later, the 458th Bomb Group, USAAF, was brought to life on an airfield in Utah and, in January 1944, its four squadrons of Liberator bombers flew, via Brazil and West Africa, from the USA to Old Catton, or, more accurately, to Horsham St Faiths Airfield. Their ground crews made their way more prosaically across the Atlantic on board the USS 'Florence Nightingale'. Although, or perhaps because, Horsham St Faiths was the only permanent RAF base used by the USAAF in Norfolk accommodation proved to be a problem; there were four squadrons of four-engined bombers and the numbers of ground crew and support staff seemed to be limitless. Additional housing was rapidly built. They chose the field alongside The White House, hastily built a concrete roadway (now called Woodland Drive), erected the nissen huts, laid on electricity and water, called it 'The Comm Site' and removed the barrier across the bottom of Taylors Lane for quick access to the airfield.

By this time the war was going well for the Allies, Italy had surrendered and the Russians were steadily reclaiming their Homeland, and the exuberance of the airmen increased the cheerfulness of the villagers. Not only that, their free and easy ways were a boon to the children. *Maire Booty:* "We children were in clover. Americans were constantly passing up and down Taylors Lane, handing out chewing gum, sweets and hard dark chocolate; officers too walked by and before long we had air-crew begging our mums to wash for them. They brought us gifts of orange juice and tinned sausage meat and, in return, we gave them hospitality, eggs, fruit and vegetables. Moreover, the children whose mothers washed for officers received frequent invitations to parties on the camp". Bicycles were in great demand by the Americans and many old bikes were renovated and sold on for them to make their way around the dispersal areas. Several of the village girls and wives found part-time or voluntary employment on the base – Doreen Earl served coffee one night a week in the base NAAFI and Mrs Wright helped man a mobile canteen.

The main source of recreation and entertainment was, of course, Norwich and again the men of the 458th Group had the advantage of being on the closest base to it, so that 'liberty trucks' were often rumbling through the village well after midnight. But if they preferred something closer at hand, there was the Saturday Night Dance in the Racquets Court. In January, 1944, the Social Services Committee in Old Catton had arranged with the military (then in full occupation of Catton Hall and its grounds) for the Parish Hall piano to be moved to the Racquets Court and for dances to be held there. Doreen Earl, when she was not engaged on ARP duties, played this piano as leader of a four piece band (piano, accordion, violin and drums) known as 'The Racqueteers'. *Eileen Fox*: "The band played on a balcony above the only entrance and their enthusiasm used to make the ceiling of the cloakroom under the balcony go up and down to the beat of the music". The dances were at first attended solely by RAF and locally billeted army personnel but quickly grew in popularity.

There was a darker side to all this activity, however. As the squadrons became operational so the number of casualties began to mount. The first plane of the 458th Group to crash fell onto Hellesdon on the 2nd March, killing seven of the crew, and three days later another came down on to Hellesdon golf course; subsequently, the village children became used to staring at returning bombers with pieces missing, 'feathered' props or firing off coloured distress flares.

The two well-recorded Liberator crashes onto Old Catton were both the result of training flights, instigated because the severe wintry weather in early 1945 had curtailed bombing missions. Any slight lull in this bad weather was used for practice flights to improve the standard of formation flying and on the 22nd of January, 1945, the Rackheath Bomb Group had just completed one such flight when the plane piloted by Flight Officer McArthur lost power on two of its engines. There was no chance that he would be able to reach St Faiths airfield and the plane just cleared the roof of the Church Street school before crashing into the woods of Catton Park and bursting into flames. Dennis Mays was at his desk in the school for afternoon lessons and saw smoke and exploding tracers rising from behind the wall in Church Street. Luckily for the village it had been a practice flight and no bombs were carried but all nine crew-men were killed. Just three weeks later, at lunch-time on the 13th February, Rosemary Shimmens was playing in the garden of the family bungalow on North Walsham Road when 'A

Dog's Life', a Liberator from the St Faiths Bomb Group struggled overhead with engine trouble and then hit and skidded down the length of the Deer Park before finally disintegrating on Spixworth Road. It too had been taking part in a practice flight and the only bombs aboard were sand filled but, nevertheless, all the crew perished, the houses on the corner of Church Street were badly damaged and one of the occupants, Mrs Bilby, was injured.

Just a month later, on March the 14th, a fully bombed-up Liberator blew up on the runway at St Faiths after being fired on accidentally by a gunner in another plane. Amazingly there were no casualties but seven other planes were damaged and most of Old Catton shook to the roar of the explosion. *Mrs Margaret Fisher:* "There was a loud explosion, all the windows in the bungalow which were open blew shut and those which were shut were blown open. My father was working at Sprowston Hall and saw the the large mushroom of smoke and rushed home to make sure we were all safe". The same explosion is understood to have blown the future Mrs Jimmy Boulter into a tree as she worked on farmland close by.

Less than two months later the war in Europe came to an end and there were again pyrotechnics at the base as the airmen fired off a profusion of flares in celebration. There were wild scenes elsewhere, too, as, for instance, in Norwich Market Place where a mass of citizens and service-men and women danced and jigged; the spire of Norwich Cathedral was illuminated by searchlights and people in Old Catton removed their blackout curtains.

In July, 1949, a plaque was placed on the wall in Church Street to record Old Catton's part in the war, and in 1950 the Parish Council had the solemn task of adding eighteen more names to the Old Catton War Memorial. Amongst these were Leslie Smith, Walter Smith (not related) and Martin Pugh all of whom had enlisted in the Royal Norfolk Regiment and had died as prisoners of war of the Japanese; Leslie Smith was the eldest son of the gardener and laundress at Catton Court, and Martin Pugh had moved to Louis Close in the 1930s and now left behind a wife and two small boys. Another name was Maxime Jollivet, a merchant navy captain who went down with his ship (the SS 'Empire Lancer'), leaving behind a wife and son living on St Clements Hill. Another name was Daphne Powles, a happy-natured girl who had lived on Longe Road but followed her elder sister into the ATS and died on an Ack-Ack site near Morecambe. World War II spread its net far and wide and not all its victims died in the heat of battle. We can only trust that no more names will need to be added in the 21st Century.

13. A group of farm workers at St Faiths Road in 1938:- Jacky Boulter, George Boulter, Arthur Wilson, Walter Gallant, Harry Hall, George Boulter Snr, Jimmy Neale, Dick Willimot, James Neale Snr, Russell White, Frank Hunt, Jimmy Boulter. Front row: Eddie Willimot, Jack Boulter and ' Tiddler' Morgan *(J Boulter).*

14. Jimmy Boulter pictured in near the Lodge gates of Catton Park with hay-cutter *(J Boulter).*

15. Workers in front of the kiln at Lodge Lane brickworks in 1936. Those present include Fred Bensley, Denny Stone, Jack Coman, Bill Fox jnr, Billy Woods, Tuffy Ellis, Arthur Chase and Stanley Woods *(D Woods)*.

16. Stanley Woods and unknown workmate digging clay at Lodge Lane in 1937 *(D Woods)*.

17. Workers in front the Lodge Lane kiln in 1937 *(D Woods)*.

18. The Badcock family, blacksmiths, at Church Street smithy at the turn of the century.   Back row: John Bly, Josh Taylor, 2 unknown workmen. Middle row: Archibald Badcock, Willam Badcock, Edward Badcock.   Front row: Geoffrey Badcock (William's grandson) *(S Currall)*.

19. Looking north from Church Street to the old smithy in 1967. At the extreme right of the picture the chimneys of Laundry Cottages can just be seen *(R Jones)*.

20. The start of construction of the new RAF station at Fifers Lane in 1939 *(Courtesy A Buxton)*.

21. Members of the ATS in the grounds of Catton Hall during Word War II.

22. An aerial view of the village in the 1930s, centred on Church Street. Catton Hall, with its park and gardens, dominates the scene: note the cricket square in the Hall grounds (right).

23. Youngsters make the most of a spell of snowy weather in the Deer Park in 1976 *(R Jones)*.

24. Catton House, seen here in 1880, was demolished in 1958 to make way for the Colkett Drive development.

25. Catton Court, St Faiths Road, on the eve of its demolition in 1986 *(Mrs Brewis)*.

AUSTERITY 1945 - 1954

The most immediate, and in many ways the most noticeable, event marking the end of the European war as far as Old Catton was concerned was the departure of the Americans from Horsham St Faiths. Their last mission had been on the 25th of April, 1945 and with typical directness their return to the States began on the 14th of June. Twenty or more aircrew were packed in to each returning Liberator whilst the ground staff made their way to Liverpool and any waiting ship. Some, however, had to remain for a while to clear the base of all warlike materials (these being returned to the main storage depot at Burtonwood, presumably for transfer to the Pacific operations area) and also for the disposal of all perishables. Some were given away, more were destroyed. A rumour persisted in Old Catton that one hundred or more bicycles had been buried in a pit on the airfield near Bullock Hill!

On the Continent, seemingly millions of people were on the move as displaced persons and ex-prisoners of war trekked back to their homelands. In Old Catton the scale was much smaller as the village witnessed the return of its fighting men and former POWs. Demobilisation took place as rapidly as the system could sustain but of course not quickly enough for those well down the list and not at all for the young soldiers being transferred to 'Tiger Force' to fight the Japanese. The newly released serviceman was readily identifiable by his new demob suit; demobilised service-women had the option of taking £12.10/- in cash and 56 clothing coupons if they felt they could do better than the outfits on offer.

Ex-prisoners of war were being brought back from the chaos of post-war Germany with great promptitude but those captured by the Japanese were having to be a little more patient. The first to land in England arrived at Southampton on the SS 'Corfu' on the 7th of October, 1945, and a few days later the 'Monowai' sailed into Liverpool, both having departed from Singapore and been routed across the Indian Ocean. Still later came other FEPOWs who were freed in Japan and were carried over the Pacific and Canada to enable them to return to their homes in the Eastern Counties. John Lane was aboard the SS 'Corfu' and the day after it docked at Southampton he arrived at Thorpe Station along with other returning Norfolk FEPOWs. Here he was met by Mr Duffield, the Old Catton garage owner and friend of the family, who intuitively had come to the station to meet him (Mr Duffield was a spiritualist) and John Lane rode the last few miles of his long journey in style in a saloon car. His main impression of Old Catton at this time was that it was "dull and drab", a reaction, perhaps, to the glaring sunlight and colours of his last three and a half years in the Far East.

Civilians, too, were on the move. Those living in temporary accommodation because they had been bombed out and those living with relations as a result of the exigencies of war were all now looking for a place of their own and were being thwarted by a desperate shortage of houses. Eventually 'Prefabs' made from aluminium originally intended for war-planes provided a short term answer but in the interim 'squatting' was the immediate solution. There were empty army camps aplenty and one of these was the 'Comm Site' off St Faiths Road, so recently vacated by the GIs, comprising American style Nissen huts clustered in groups of three, each group with a common entrance. It was difficult to know how to treat the squatters and they themselves usually moved on but, in 1948, the St Faiths and Aylsham Rural District Council officially assumed responsibility, named the site Woodland Drive and designated some of the huts as temporary council houses. One of the families provided with accommodation at this site was that of *Mrs Edwards*: "We had been bombed out of our London home and had moved to my grandmother's in Cawston – and had been surprised by the basic style of country life! In 1949 we were allocated a hut at Woodland Drive. There were about fifty families living there, one family per hut, and each hut had a living room with an open fire, a kitchen with a coal-fired cooking range and a copper, and three bedrooms; the main drawback was that all the huts suffered badly from condensation". The wives of RAF officers were at that time living in caravans on the meadow that is now Catton Chase. Later on, in 1952, the erection of permanent council houses in Woodland Drive was considered but snags over ownership of the huts, road and land led to the idea being abandoned, although the families were eventually moved out (many of them to Tills Road) to make way for permanent housing.

Social life in the village took a step towards normality when the army returned the Parish Hall to the village in the spring of 1946; the Parish Hall Committee had its first post-war meeting in the building on the 30th of May, 1946, under the Chairmanship of Mr Fred Booty. Unexpected help in the return of the Hall had been received from the Norwich Education Committee which was anxious to use it and its kitchen for the provision of school dinners and was prepared to pay an annual rental of £26 for the privilege. More financial aid for the Hall was forthcoming from the military who agreed to pay £40 as compensation for 'war damage' and the amenities were improved when the YMCA donated a piano and two surplus tea urns were purchased from the WVS.

Then on June 8th, 1946, a fine summer's day, the village officially celebrated the end of the war with a Sports Afternoon. This had been organised by the Parish Council, complete with teas and refreshments, and took place on the meadow behind the school; it was attended by 120 children, including those from the RAF married quarters in Fifers Lane. In a way the RAF reciprocated when they invited the public to attend the first Open Day to be held at Horsham St Faiths.

This was on the 12th of September, 1946, and started an annual event that was to endure until the end of the 1950s. The RAF had repossessed the airfield in July, 1945, and were now flying the new jet planes in and out of the base and, in fact, seven Meteors took part in the fly-past during this first Open Day.

The fighting may have finished but signs of the war were still evident in Norfolk. German prisoners of war, working on the farms, were not all repatriated until May, 1948, and Italian POWs, very noticeable by their blue uniforms with an orange sun on the back, were content to carry on working here and ran their own small camps on the edge of Mousehold and along Salhouse Road. Royal Engineers continued to clear the beaches of obstructions and mines. Rationing was still a fact of life and, indeed, took a turn for the worse when bread was added to the list of rationed goods in July, 1946; although in Old Catton a welcome opportunity to augment the ration materialised when The White House was turned into a chicken-rearing station. *Eileen Grant:* "I used to queue up at Woolsey's Farm to buy day-old chicks for rearing when we had a broody hen, the family's egg allocation being surrendered in order to obtain chicken food. My mother boiled kitchen scraps like potato peelings to supplement their feed and we kept surplus eggs in isinglass". But in a perverse sort of way rationing gave a feeling of security and well-being to everybody – there was full employment but little opportunity to spend – and summer holidays became a way of frittering away some of the spare cash, especially as Cromer beach had been cleared. And it *was* a fine summer in 1946!

In Old Catton a new and popular form of entertainment was accessible by walking down Taylors Lane (now re-opened by the Air Ministry) and along Fifers Lane to the Firs Speedway which was attracting crowds of 10,000 to 12,000. The standard of living in the village was also somewhat improved by the appearance of a telephone box in October, 1946, in Spixworth Road (where it stands to this day) and a limited scheme of street lighting in 1947. But general shortages of all sorts of commodities made life a little more difficult and the desperate winter of 1946/47 added to the stresses and strains, everything was in short supply except snow drifts! Thereafter, circumstances began to improve. A fine summer in 1947 was enhanced by the cricketing triumphs of Dennis Compton and Norfolk's Bill Edrich, and the next year saw not only the Olympic Games being held in London but also the abolition of bread and potato rationing. A new general store appeared in Spixworth Road (at what is now No. 202) but Mrs Cracknell, its owner, was unable to make a success of it and within a few years it had closed down. Perhaps shoppers preferred the greater choice available in the City and certainly this was now more accessible as the 93 bus service was expanded in May, 1950, by the addition of double decker buses to the route.

In one respect, however, the village was still suffering from the effects of the war. It had not recovered from the loss of its sporting facilities. The cricket pitch in Catton Park had been ploughed up as part of the war effort, no real attempt was being made to revive the clubs, and the tennis courts at The White House had disappeared. Still at least the Parish Council was searching around for ways and means of providing a recreation ground.

In 1949, the devaluation of the £ helped to boost our exports and the standard of living in England again took an upturn, and the same year brought the first signs of the development and expansion of Old Catton. All the large houses in the village had been standing empty and dilapidated since the end of the war and they were ripe for development. The first to receive attention was Eastwood House which, in 1949, was taken over by Trevor, Page and Co of Queen Street, Norwich as a furniture depository and the conversion was accompanied by the wholesale felling of the woods around the house. The White House was bought by Mr Musselwhite, who re-named it Wolsey House, and turned it into a chicken-rearing station, while Mr Tom Pointer bought The Elms in order to expand his holdings. Most importantly, the link between Old Catton and Catton Hall was broken when, in 1948, Norfolk County Council bought the then empty Hall, together with the surrounding gardens and woods, for conversion into an old people's home.

EXPANSION   1954 AND ONWARDS

These were the years that saw the transformation of Old Catton from a village dominated by its mansions and mini-estates to a desirable residential suburb of the city of Norwich. It was, after all, only three miles from the city centre and with the growing use of the car and the increasing frequency of the bus services this proved to be no distance at all. The affluence and confidence generated by the Macmillan government promoted a housing boom in the County and it was inevitable that 'hungry' developers scouring the area for suitable building land would fasten on Old Catton where the scattering of large and empty houses, together with their spacious grounds, proved to be an irresistible attraction.

But ahead of them came the Old Catton landowners themselves. Prominent amongst these was the Buxton family who had already instigated a modest amount of post-war building at Partridge Way and continued to develop odd corners of their estate by building small clusters of refined houses. In 1954 they cleared the woods at the top of Church Street to make way for those houses behind the high brick wall and, in 1955, the scrubland opposite the school was cleared to enable Park Close to be built. In 1957 Mr Buxton notified his allotment holders that he intended to 'flip over' the allotments that lined Fifers Lane to the field behind so that the frontage thus freed could be used for housing. It was not all plain sailing, however, for later that year he was refused permission to build at the bottom of the Back Road and, in 1959, he was similarly prevented from building on Butter Close, a meadow which later became the Recreation Ground. But in 1967 approval was given for the building of the Hall School (then known as a Junior Training Centre) and for a children's hostel and houses which would form Parkside Drive. Between 1969 and 1972 the Estate orchards and the old Laundry were developed and became part of Garrick Green and in 1973 the School Pasture was sold to Riley Builders who built not only Blacksmiths Way there but also converted the old smithy area to housing. A major transaction involving the Catton Hall estate was the sale to Norwich City Council, in 1974, of those fields and woods on the western side of St Faiths Road stretching up towards Partridge Way. This in due time became the Fiddlewood housing estate, all within the confines of a City boundary that had been extended in 1967 to take in the airfield.

One casualty of this last development was Old Catton's residential tramp. This was 'Cutty' – his real name was not known nor any aspect of his past life. He had taken up residence in the woods alongside St Faiths Road after being displaced from his post-war abode (by the building of the Vulcan Road industrial estate) and Mr

Buxton allowed him to make use of the water tap on the nearby allotments. To the chagrin of the allotment-holders, 'Cutty' deduced from this that he was also entitled to help himself to vegetables being grown there! However, the old tramp was eventually caught up in the regulated life of officialdom and was taken away by Norfolk Social Services to a residential home.

Meanwhile the break-up of the other large parcels of land within the village proceeded and, in the south eastern corner, **Catton House** was being transformed. This handsome mansion, described as brick built and plastered in the Italianate style, stood on the hill overlooking Reeve's Meadow and Oak Lane amidst 32 acres of farmland, parkland and gardens which extended down to where Carterford Drive now is. There were 8ft high yew hedges lining each side of the drive leading to the house and a quarter acre lawn in front of it. At the beginning of the century the house was occupied by Lieut-Col. Sir Edward Mansel and his wife, Lady Julia Mansel, with servants living on the top floor, and with the main lodge on Spixworth Road and another one on Oak Lane (both occupied by gardeners). The colonel died in 1908 but Lady Julia continued to live in the house until her death in June, 1944, with (it is said) a small pearl-handled revolver by her bedside.

By the end of 1944 the house had been acquired by the Norwich Union in order to house staff returning from wartime relocation to Buxton in Derbyshire, while awaiting repossession of their Norfolk homes. The house was converted into a dozen flats and a large communal kitchen was created on the ground floor. Ten years later the few remaining residents were re-located and it was finally used, under Red Cross supervision, to house 30 Hungarian refugees of the 1956 uprising. Just two years before that event, a tentative development of the grounds began with the building of houses along the Spixworth Road frontage and then, in 1956, Oak Lane was developed and Mansel Drive was created – followed in 1959 by Carterford Drive, Pembrey Close and Swinburne Close. Finally, the House, already damaged by fire, was itself demolished (along with the two lodges) to make way for Colkett Drive which was completed sometime in 1961.

On the opposite side of Spixworth Road was the lodge and drive leading to **Eastwood House** which was, in fact, situated quite close to Constitution Hill and presided over a smaller and more compact estate. In the early years of the century it was owned by William Howlett, and later by his son Neville who owned the piano shop in London Street, Norwich. Neville Howlett never married but was a keen sportsman, being captain of Catton Cricket Club and a valued member of Catton Bowls Club – there was a bowling green in the grounds of the house – and he often arranged fetes and sports meetings on his land.

Like Catton House it was used by the army during the war and remained rather dilapidated until taken over by Trevor, Page and Co Ltd of Norwich as a furniture depository during the early 1950s. In 1954 a small development along

Spixworth Road and the old drive began to take shape followed by houses fronting Constitution Hill from the ring road to English Road and, eventually, a small frontage on that ring road. The ring road had been planned and surveyed in 1958 so, as the grounds of both Eastwood House and Catton House were developed, a broad swathe of land was reserved for this. Just into Sprowston, the grounds belonging to Meadow House (now the Veterinary Clinic) and the erstwhile RAF Old Catton had also been developed – with the exception of the bunker and the base of the old guard-room which still exist! So the change of landscape was complete in this part of Old Catton.

On the other side of the village, the extensive acres belonging to **Crome House** were on the change. At the beginning of the century the house had been known as Gardenhurst and was owned by Mr Hanning-Lee but the name was changed in the twenties when Mr Fred Gough moved in. He owned the Norwich Cardboard and Box Co and was a keen member of the Norwich Aero Club; it was said that he kept an aeroplane of his in the paddock behind the house. After the war the Gough family moved back briefly into the house but by 1956 it had become a boarding house with 17 caravans in the paddocks (for a time some of these were occupied by wives of the RAF officers stationed at Horsham St Faiths). Just previously, in 1954, houses were built along the St Faiths Road frontage and the orchards behind were sold to Mr Landamore who took up residence there in a shack. It was he who sold this land for the building of Catton Chase and Chase Close, and when the stable block and coach house were demolished in 1960, housing extended further along St Faiths Road, the old roadside drainage pond being filled in for this purpose. By this time Catton Chase was almost complete and a commercial aspect was added when planning permission was given for the row of shops. Meanwhile, Crome House itself had reverted once more to a family dwelling and Dr Brewis moved in to open the village's first surgery. That was in 1966 and a mere two years later the first floor was converted to flats with the surgery continuing to operate on the ground floor until it moved to a purpose built health centre in Lodge Lane. The house survives to this day despite a serious fire in 1994 and stands impressively open to the road in contrast to the days when it was barely visible through a belt of trees.

Its neighbour, **The Red House**, is also a survivor in much diminished circumstances. It lost its kitchen gardens to the bungalows of Catton Chase in 1962/3 and in 1962 its rear gardens were sold off for more building works and quickly evolved into Lancaster Close. Of all the village 'mansions' this is arguably the one that most ordinary people would have chosen to live in. With its tree-fringed formal garden and lawn at the front, its greenhouses behind the coach-houses in Taylors Lane and its kitchen garden running along the south side down to the meadow at the rear, it was of a manageable size. The rear garden had a fine shrubbery bordering the tennis lawn and led on to the orchards along the edge of the meadow. This late Victorian house was well planned, with a central heating system, wash basins and fitted wardrobes in the bedrooms, and a maid's quarters (complete with bathroom and toilet) accessible only by a staircase from the kitchen and thus separate from the rest of the house. Mr Finch, a director of the Norwich brewery, Steward and Patteson, moved into this fine house in 1909 and was followed in the 1930s by Mr Wilford, personnel manager of Mann Egerton, and like Mr Gough, his neighbour, a keen member of the Norwich Aero Club. The Wilford family moved out in 1939 but the house returned to residential use after the war and at one time was occupied by the FitzMaurice family. Only recently has it become the home of a religious foundation.

On the opposite side of the road, **The Elms** survives obscurely behind its belt of trees. It started life as an Elizabethan farmhouse, was rebuilt in Georgian times and finally, at the end of the nineteenth century, had a spacious wing added on the south side. At the end of the war the house was empty and dilapidated and was bought in 1946 by Mr Tom Pointer who converted the badminton and croquet lawns into ornamental gardens. He applied, unsuccessfully, for permission to develop the frontage on St Faiths Road in 1959 and then, in 1983, he sold the property to developers. But the grounds associated with the house were not extensive and the small group of houses in the corner of the junction of Lodge Lane and St Faiths Road is the only tangible evidence of the developers' labours. Not unnaturally these houses are collectively known as The Elms and quite by chance have caused a reversion of local history as the service road they stand upon follows the original road line, the one which was deflected by earlier owners of The Elms to ensure their privacy. The house itself, for the remaining years of the century, became the offices of the Wherry Housing Association for a while and is now the home of Age Concern..

Two hundred yards down the road was **The White House**, or Wolsey House as it later became. In its heyday it was a desirable dwelling and Maire Booty recalls being told by an old lady who had been governess to the children of the British Consul in Rome that, each summer, the Consul's family would spend their vacation with the Steward family in the White House. Mrs Steward was the aunt of the Consul's wife. Every Sunday the two families would go to St Margaret's Church in their carriages. The Steward family left the village in the 1920s and Mr Woolsey, another solicitor, and his family moved in. He was a bit of a character and installed a large aviary at the front of the house (screened by a belt of trees) wherein the birds had plenty of opportunity to fly and he was often seen walking in the neighbourhood with his pet parrot on his shoulder. His wife also was a little unconventional and established herself as a village philanthropist. She encouraged the local tennis club to use the court belonging to the house, she was very active in the newly formed Women's Institute, invited the Girl Guides to meet in her library and make use of the paddock at the rear of the house and, in the early days of the war, she organised the knitting of gloves and balaclavas, rolling of bandages and even the collection of scrap metal. However, towards the end of 1940 the Woolsey family left the village and for the rest of the war the house was used by the army. Not only that, a large part of its land was compulsorily purchased in 1943 for the building of the USAAF 'Comm Site'. The post-war plan to build council houses here never came to fruition and Riley Builders finally acquired the site and started building the bungalows of Woodland Drive in 1956. The house itself was bought by Mr Musselwhite who established a chicken sexing and rearing business there and, in 1962, converted the upper floor into flats. Wolsey House was becoming increasingly run down and in 1967 a large piece of its land was sold for the development of Players Way and, within a relatively short period of time, the house was demolished, along with Catton Court, to be replaced by the retirement homes complex.

Catton Court, the neighbouring property, at the turn of the century was the home of Mr Bullard of Bullard's Brewery. He was succeeded by Colonel Currie, whose son died somewhat bizarrely of an infection contracted at the dentist; when the colonel himself died his widow and daughter continued to live there until 1958 at which time Colonel Hogan and family moved in. In 1962 the cottages belonging to the house and lining St Faiths Road (one of these being Blanche Pye's old home) were demolished and new houses built on the site and in 1967 the paddock was absorbed as part of the Players Way development whilst the adjoining meadow became part of Garrick Green. The old house, however, lived on until it too was demolished in October 1986 to make way for the Catton Court Retirement complex. Now, only the coach houses, which had been bought by a local plumber and used as workshops, remain.

Not far away, in Church Street, **The Manor House** had to be content with only a limited contribution to the expansion of the village as most of its land had been sold off before the start of the century. After Mrs Crampton's death Mr Albert Cubitt, the Norwich antique dealer, had rented it and, indeed, throughout the war had had to share it with billeted service personnel. He would have happily bought the old house but for legal complications arising with the Crampton family. When he eventually moved out it was converted into three flats, and subsequently into two houses, whilst the garden was sold in 1962 to enable two pleasant houses to be built on St Faiths Road. The coach house was transformed into a house and a bungalow built close to it in 1960.

On Spixworth Road, **The Beeches** made its contribution towards the expansion of the village when, in 1958, a large part of its secluded garden and its bowling green was sold off to be developed as Beeches Close. This pleasantly modest house was home to Mrs Edward Buxton after her husband died in 1929 but for most of the inter-war period it belonged to the Bunting family (of Buntings Department Store) and Mrs Bunting continued to live there during the war. It, happily, survives.

Not so lucky was **The Warren**, to which Rear Admiral Sir Edward Berry retired in 1814. He was one of Nelson's favourite captains and took part in both the Battle of the Nile and Trafalgar and is reputed to have had part of the garden laid out in the form of a ship's quarter deck. By the 1930s the house was occupied by the Morse family and the gardens are remembered by Iris Youngman, (whose family lived opposite in a terraced cottage), as being pretty, well laid out and including tennis courts and a revolving summerhouse, all concealed behind a high plain wall. Like many other Old Catton houses it was used by the army during the war but then was bought by Captain Palmer, a rodent control officer of St Faiths and Aylsham RDC. His application to demolish the house in 1965 was granted and in 1966 the group of houses known as The Warren began to take shape.

Further along Spixworth Road is **Greyfriars** which also contributed to the expansion of Old Catton at this time but managed to survive, although in a truncated form. The house first came into prominence as the home of George Lindley, a successful nurseryman in the late 18th Century. His eldest son, in due course, was even better known, becoming the first Professor of Botany at London University, helping to establish Kew Gardens and being called in as an adviser on the Irish Potato Famine of 1845. In the early 20th Century the house was the home of Louis Tillett, a prominent Norwich Solicitor and known as "the poor man's lawyer". It was his custom to open the gardens of the house on Sundays during the summer and many residents of the area would take a Sunday stroll around Old Catton and visit these gardens to admire the flowers and shrubs and, in the greenhouses and hot houses, the exotic fruits. After Mr Tillett moved out, the Revd Copeman moved in, for a while, and older villagers remember the lending library that his daughters organised in the coach house. During the war the house was extensively used – billeting troops, training the local Home Guard and acting as an ARP headquarters. Maire Booty remembers going there as a Girl Guide and being paid 2d an evening to be bandaged up by trainee ARP wardens anxious to learn their First Aid techniques. By 1945 it was looking decidedly run down and in 1950 it was bought by Mr Ken Worship, managing director of Laurence, Scott and Electromotors, and completely restored by Bush Builders. The attached servants' quarters on the north side were demolished and the stable block was converted into an attractive house, now Hunters Lodge, for Walter Klinge, a Danish citizen temporarily working for Bush Builders. Greyfriars was restored to something of its former splendour and Mr Worship made good use of it to entertain prospective customers, converting the cellar into a well equipped bar. Unfortunately the Worship family moved on and the house once more declined. A small part of the gardens had been lost in the 1930s when numbers 129 and 131 Spixworth Road were built and now, in 1969, the ornamental gardens, those same gardens that had been so popular on pre-war Sunday afternoons, were sold and developed as Greyfriars Close; the final blow came in 1981 when the woods that had formed the western edge of the property were sold to provide an extension to the new recreation ground. The old house itself narrowly missed being demolished when, in 1970, a planning application was submitted to build a supermarket on this site. It was rejected by both Parish and District Councils despite the almost complete absence of shops in the village.

Shops had been slow in coming to the village. The cluster on the George Hill crossroads had remained as the sole representative of retailing ventures for over half a century until joined by the NAAFI on the opposite side of the village. This was a by-product of RAF Horsham St Faiths, and when the RAF left in 1963 the shop stayed – at first to serve only the airmen's families in Fifers Lane but, eventually, to open its doors to all-comers. For a short while also, as previously mentioned, Mrs Cracknell opened her shop in Spixworth Road but the village did not get a permanent shop at its centre until February, 1958, when Mr Clabon obtained permission to convert his bungalow at the corner of Woodland Drive. He had hoped to include a post office but, despite numerous letters to the Head Postmaster in Norwich, the postal authorities remained convinced that Mr Carver's post office on North Walsham Road and the one at Catton Grove were more than adequate to cover the village. A year later another shop opened, this time in Burma Road, and, ironically, this was awarded the coveted post office licence when Mr Carver retired in 1964; it continued to function as a general store and post office for some years but eventually slimmed down to pure post office as it is today. In 1967 an application for a small parade of shops at the entrance to Catton Chase was approved, after being rejected by the planners for at least 10 years.

By this time supermarkets were springing up in Norwich and came near to Old Catton when Mr and Mrs Bugden converted their popular shop on Wroxham Road into a supermarket in 1974. But after the rejected plan for Greyfriars, similar proposals for supermarkets in Proctor Road and then in White Woman Lane were successively defeated in 1973 and 1974 and Old Catton did not get its own supermarket until February, 1980, when Keymarkets (later Somerfield) opened as part of a modest shopping precinct on the edge of The Paddocks development. Even so the approval for this was given with considerable apprehension by the Parish Council. Would the store be too big? Would heavy delivery lorries swamp the village? Where would the customers come from? They need not have worried about the customers for on the first late-night opening (until 8pm) queues at the checkouts wound all around the gangways and were not cleared until about 10pm!

No doubt many of these shoppers came from Sprowston, Spixworth and further afield but Old Catton itself was continuing to expand. The large old houses and their gardens had been exploited and the market gardens and nurseries that had been such a feature of the village were not to escape the same fate. The first to go was Tills Farm, sold to Mr Moore who promptly proceeded to build Moore Avenue on these fields in the 1950s. All the land on the eastern side of Spixworth Road, between The Tills and White Woman Lane, had at one time been part of the massive Cozens-Hardy estate that stretched from Wroxham Road to Spixworth Road and from Allens Lane almost to Beeston St Andrew. Interestingly though, a square of land in the middle of this is shown on an 1860s map as 'Betts' Field'. By the 1930s the fields bordering Spixworth Road, including one belonging to Greyfriars, had been sold off and some building had occurred there before the war. More land was developed after the war and by 1956 Burma Road was in place. It was in 1957 that the link-up between this and Moore Avenue was sanctioned by the Rural District Council, with the confident pronouncement that through traffic would never use this link to any extent!

In 1967 further substantial inroads into the Cozens-Hardy estate were made when Norfolk Garden Estates purchased the land that was to become Proctor Road and environs and this was followed by the sale of Betts' Field to the same company allowing that whole area to be developed by 1973. In 1974 Wilcon Builders added the final fringe along Spixworth Road.

The other large landowner in the village was the Norman Trust which owned large swathes of land north of Lodge Lane and White Woman Lane. As we have seen, a small part of this was sold off pre-war to allow the council houses in White Woman Lane to be built but otherwise Alderman Norman's land was largely intact. In the early years of the 20th Century **The Old Hall**, where Alderman John Norman had lived in the early 1700s (and where Samuel Bignold had lived briefly in the early 1800s) had declined to a farm house occupied by farmer Tallowin and later by Frank Gowing, another farmer and also a landowner, and deteriorated still further during and after World War II. In 1988, however, it was bought by Roger Cawdron, a prominent Norwich licensee and restaurateur who renovated it and turned it into a select and unobtrusive guest house. By this time the farm-land once associated with the old house had long gone. In 1966 the Norman Trustees were intent on selling a large tract of land for housing and, by 1968, these fields blossomed into Three Corner Drive and The Paddocks. Just a year later another land deal was set up and Norman Drive and West Acre Drive began to take shape.

This left Pointer's Farm (to the south of Lodge Lane and west of St Faiths Road) as the only farm-land still within the boundaries of Old Catton and here too the developers were closing in. In 1986 the first of a scheduled 156 houses began the formation of Priors Drive and, in the very last year of the century, work started on Old Lodge Tye where 179 houses will cover the last of those arable lands that formed such a feature of Old Catton life in the early years of the century, taking away almost the last major industrial activity in the village, Pointers extensive poultry processing works.

This great growth of houses inevitably began to pull the centre of the village northwards and additional services were needed to cater for all these new villagers. The Lodge Lane brickworks closed down in 1968 and within a year or so the site was snapped up by Norfolk County Council to provide the land for a brand new primary school. In 1980 a new supermarket and a small parade of shops were built on the northern edge of The Paddocks, accompanied by another small development of houses. A modern surgery appeared on newly available land opposite the Lodge Lane School in 1990 and in September, 1996, the new and long promised Recreation Ground was formally opened on the opposite side of Spixworth Road. Lastly, there had been for some years concern that the churchyard at St Margaret's was reaching its capacity. The Parish Council eventually negotiated the sale of an acre of land on St Faiths Road near to the airfield for use as the Parish Cemetery and this was consecrated by the Bishop of Lynn in a raging snowstorm on the 23rd January, 1984, in the presence of local clergy and councillors. Schooling, shopping, leisure, sickness and death all catered for!

EXPANSION - THE FIGURES

The 1891 Census disclosed that there were approximately 220 houses in Catton. 80 or so of these, in Rackham Fields, Catton Grove and St Clements Hill, were lost as a result of the boundary changes of 1907, the Norwich (Extension) Order. By 1939 the number had been restored to about 220 and remained so until the early 1950s. Between 1950 and 1975 approximately 1180 houses were built and by 1998 this figure had risen to 2300.

The 1931 population figures of Catton and its neighbouring parishes set out below provide an interesting commentary on the perceived view of Catton as a Norfolk village rather than a Norwich suburb.

	Catton	Sprowston	Hellesdon
1911	634	906	826
1931	609	2109	2237

In the second half of the century, however, Old Catton joined the rest in the race for growth and towards the end of the century (1991) the parish population had risen to 5,700.

THE GOVERNANCE OF OLD CATTON

THE PARISH COUNCIL

The inaugural meeting of Catton Parish Council was held on the 20th December, 1894, following a Parish meeting on the 4th December when eleven candidates were chosen by a show of hands. Prior to this date infrequent parish meetings had been held but all records of such occasions have been lost.

This first council comprised:- Mr Donald Steward of The White House, St Faiths Road (also manager of Steward and Patteson's brewery) who became the Council Chairman, Mr Harry Gurney Buxton of Catton Hall who became the Council's first Clerk, Mr Archie Badcock, of Church Street, who was the Parish Overseer as well as the village blacksmith, Mr Henry Batchelor of Church Street, a gardener, Mr Benjamin Bevan of Spixworth Road, a solicitor, Mr William Walton of 3, Catton Grove Villas, an accountant, Mr Robert Guymer of Spixworth Road and of 'independent means', Mr Dennington of Spixworth Road, a market gardener, Mr Walter Dack of Church Street, a wheelwright, Mr William Gee of Branksome, Spixworth Road, a solicitor, and a Mr Ambrose Bell. Within a short time Harry Buxton went abroad and William Walton became Clerk.

The Council's second meeting was to submit 'suitable' names for the post of Parish Constable (an unpaid position) and Mr Charles Betts was appointed. The Constable was responsible to the Parish Overseer whose duties included "relief of the necessitous", the giving of orders for medical relief, procuring rate books and collecting the parish rates, listing those persons qualified to serve as jurors, and drawing up lists of voters. The Overseer was appointed by the St Faith's Union (later the Rural District Council) and Mr Badcock served in this unpaid position for some years but, paradoxically, his Assistant (Mr Attoe) was paid to the extent of £15 per annum – presumably he undertook most of the clerical duties and was reimbursed accordingly.

Early minutes of Council meetings, hand-written in an exercise book, show it to have been concerned with two important issues – putting the Parish Charities in order and getting cover for any possible outbreak of fire. A report in the Eastern Daily Press, during 1896, that the Norwich Fire Brigade had refused to attend a serious fire in Colney because it was outside the city boundary so alarmed the Catton Council that they considered buying a fire appliance; but, in the end, they agreed to pay £14 per annum for the services of Norwich's second engine. The more minor problems causing the Council concern included faults in the roads and footpaths, drainage problems and street lighting – not that there was any but the Council was constantly writing to successive owners of The Old House in Spixworth Road reminding them of an undertaking "to light the gas lamp outside the front door on dark evenings in order to illuminate the road".

At first, the whole Council was elected annually by a show of hands at the Annual Parish Meeting until the Tenure of Office Act in 1900 made parish elections obligatory every three years. Two years before this, in January, 1898, the first Council Chairman, Mr Donald Steward, died and it is indicative of the respect in which he was held, both in the village and in Norwich, that St Margaret's Church was filled to overflowing at his funeral. Interestingly, the Council, although all male, invited Mrs Steward to join them to take her husband's place. She declined and it was not until some fifty years later that our first lady councillor, Mrs Newton, of Louis Close and nominated by the Women's Institute, took her seat. In 1901, Mr Capps of Rackham Fields became the Council Clerk and kept this post until the boundary change in 1907; his tenure of office was a great boon to researchers as he left a diligently written record of the meetings in the minute book, in copper-plate handwriting. The handwriting of the later clerks gradually deteriorated until, in the late 1960s, the minutes were typed.

The boundary dispute of the 1900s provoked several agitated Council meetings. The City was seeking to gain 219 acres from the Parish and, at some stage had stated that "Catton's system of drainage is bad and the part known as Rackham Fields is a source of danger to the city as fevers constantly break out there and spread into the city". One resident stated at a General Parish Meeting "I am opposed to any attempt to drag us from our high state of health and happiness to the lower level of increased rates and the dangers of bad smells arising from the city sewers". Another averred that having lived for thirty years in the city and twelve in comparatively salubrious Catton his "nasal organ tells me plainly when I pass from the city to the county boundary". Whilst Mr Walter Hines said he had lived for twenty years in Rackham Fields and his health could compare favourably with that of most people in Norwich. All this was to no avail, save that the new boundary followed the southern edges of the Eastwood and Catton House estates rather than going down George Hill and Oak Lane as originally proposed; but the village still lost 167 acres to its neighbour.

As a result of this change in boundary, the wages of the Assistant Overseer were reduced to £14 per annum and, a somewhat small consolation for the Council, the annual fee for the use of Norwich's second fire engine was also reduced.

Towards the end of 1919 the Council gained a permanent home when Mr Buxton transferred the Museum to them, to act as a parish hall, at a nominal rent of 1/- per annum and, as the 1920s progressed, the Council became a well-established and settled body. Many of the members served for long spells and the names of Bill English, Fred Eke, Geoffrey Badcock, Fred Day, Reggie Sabberton, Billy

Seagrove and Fred Booty recur in the Council minutes time after time during the 1920s and 30s and even, in one case, up to the 1970s. In 1928 the Council was informed that its Clerk was entitled to a remuneration of £7.10/- per year; the Clerk in question declined the offer and from that time until the retirement of Fred Booty from that post (in 1969, after 35 years service) the position remained a voluntary one. Mr Terry Fenn then became our first remunerated Clerk with an annual salary of £104.

In the early 1930s the Council was increasingly concerned with schemes for street lighting, a playing field, surface water drainage problems and a mains sewage scheme and it even became involved with the village school when one of its number was invited to become a school governor. The association with the school continued during World War II and one tenuous example is recorded in the Council minutes of April, 1942, when the Council organised a collection of used razor blades for the war effort and agreed that the proceeds should be passed to the school. Another, more sombre, wartime entry occurred in April, 1944, noting a request to the police to discourage girls from hanging around the airfield gates on Fifers Lane and Taylors Lane. The Parish Council, during the war, had been deprived of its usual meeting place, for the Parish Hall, along with Catton Hall, had been commandeered by the army: they had to make do with one of the rooms in the school, sitting cramped up on the childrens' chairs. It was not until the spring of 1946 that they were able to re-occupy the Parish Hall – only to find the building badly in need of repair and restoration. One of the Council's first tasks from its regained seat of government was the supervising of the distribution of Commonwealth food gifts to the poor and elderly of the village in that year of 1946.

The need for repair, restoration and improvement permeated the whole village and the Council now had its busiest of times as it wrestled with the post war demands for a better standard of living. The upgrading of a very modest form of street lighting installed in 1947 was a serious budgeting item as was the provision of a recreation ground for, in both cases, the costs would devolve onto the Council. New street lights were installed in 1957 and the minutes record that "were it not for the income generated by the airmen's married quarters on Fifers Lane the village would not have been able to afford the scheme". Roads were changing, footpaths and pavements needed upgrading. The village was also plagued by surface water problems – not so surprising since age old ditches and drainage ponds were being filled in by developers with little thought as to why they were there! The most serious spots were at the end of Church Street where the drains no longer fed into the old pond and, later, at the junction of Lodge Lane and Three Corner Drive where the drainage pond had been completely filled in. A brief and cheerful interlude was presented in 1953 when the Council took the lead in organising Coronation celebrations in the village.

It was in 1957, too, that an important change was signalled for the Parish Hall. Mr Desmond Buxton decided to extinguish his tenuous ownership of this hall and offered the Parish Council the outright ownership of it, together with the skating rink, for £100. The offer was speedily accepted but it was not until February, 1959, that the Council successfully negotiated the necessary loan and was able to actually purchase the building and its surrounds. Then, in conjunction with the Parish Hall trustees, the hall was completely refurbished, including replacing the open fire by oil-fired central heating and providing proper toilets to replace those two wooden huts half concealed in the trees by the skating rink. A year later, on the 13th December, 1960, the keys were formally handed over by Mr Buxton and the village had its own new and improved social centre. The building had been used in this way since 1919 and now became even more popular as a meeting place for all the local clubs and societies, Women's Institute, Horticultural Club, Girl Guides, British Legion. In 1961 a monthly Child Welfare Clinic was started here, Hazel Betts becoming its long-serving voluntary organiser, and in 1962 the village Playgroup was formed here, the first such playgroup in the County.

In 1954 the Council received significant recognition from the Rural District Council when that body began sending details of planning schemes relevant to Old Catton and a further advance was made in 1968 when the Council persuaded the Rural District Council to send planning proposals before approval so that the Council could make their comments. This input into local planning matters came just in time for the major housing developments of the 70s and 80s and, no doubt, lessened the impact of these schemes on the existing villagers. (Incidentally, this was not the first interest that the Council had had in housing for in the minutes of August, 1903, it was reported that "new houses are being erected in Spixworth Road, plans having been laid before St Faiths Council and Approved" – these were the terraced houses near The Oaks.) With the arrival of the new post-war housing came the demand for a new school and a modern sewage system. The Norfolk Education Committee took over the school and built two new classrooms in 1955, followed by three new schools in the 1970s. The sewage problem was one for the Rural District Council and a complete new system was installed in 1962. The recreation ground project was successfully concluded in 1967 following Mr Buxton's sale of Butter Close to the Parish Council in 1964. The old meadow was transformed into a very pleasant landscaped recreational area for the village with football pitches, tennis courts and a bowling green and served the growing population well. However, the population continued to grow and by the late 1980s the Parish Council was searching around for ways of expanding the facilities. An obvious solution, by purchasing the adjoining allotments, was thwarted by the reluctance of the allotment holders to move and, in 1992, the Parish Council purchased land in the north of the village which, on the 8th September, 1996, was formally opened and became Lavaré Park. The surface water drainage improvements had to wait much longer and were not started until 1986, in Oak Lane (where typically the construction of the ring road had disrupted the original drainage) and was then extended to Spixworth Road in 1989 and 1990, and later to Lodge Lane and elsewhere. Even as the century drew to a close the last section of St Faiths Road still awaited its improvements.

From its beginning in 1894, the Council had always been an independent body, its members relying on their personal reputations in the village when elections were due. In fact elections were rarely held after the 'three year tenure' legislation was introduced, nominations for the seats never exceeding the number needed. It was not until the early 1970s that party politics began to creep into local government, and it is to be wondered what our early councillors would have made of today's elections, with their propaganda from the various political parties and their determination to 'gain control'. Council meetings today, with their reports from sub-committees, long lists of items of expenditure and submissions of planning applications and tree surgery are far removed from the comfortable meetings of the early part of the century. In those early days, too, every Council meeting ended with effusive words of thanks to their Chairman – "Revd Hodgson proposed and Mr Gee seconded a hearty vote of thanks to the Chairman, and expressed, on behalf of the Council, their pleasure in having him to preside over them".

BOUNDARIES

Like other local fringe parishes, Old Catton has been wary of being swamped by Norwich ever since the mid nineteenth century when the city started its period of rapid expansion and the rows of terraced houses spread out beyond the city walls. For Old Catton the alarm bells started ringing in 1904 when the City Fathers began looking somewhat enviously at the quiet fields beyond Magdalen Road and Angel Road and proposed to take them into the City. The Norwich Extension Order came into effect on the 9th November, 1907, and the City gained Rackham Fields, Catton Grove and its environs, Elm Grove Lane and Attoe's Loke. The population of Old Catton was almost halved down to 634 but the Parish Council was not unduly distressed as the bulk of this loss was of the poorer housing in Rackham Fields and the only lost prestige housing was that at Catton Grove; there was, however, the loss of land which the Council had been hiring from the Grove Estate as allotments – interestingly allotments still exist there.

In 1933 a statutory attempt by Norwich to absorb Old Catton was rejected by Parliament and the city seemed then to abandon its territorial claims in this direction, perhaps deflected by the burgeoning success of its new council housing estates. So many houses were built at Mile Cross, Lakenham, Earlham and the like that by the mid-century the city's housing stock had been increased by nearly 50%.

Even so, by the 1950s the demand for new houses was renewed (it was, nationally, the time of a governmental drive for new housing) and Old Catton once more came under scrutiny. This renewed civic interest was stimulated by the successful development of an industrial estate along Fifers Lane and the new Vulcan Road and the realisation that the upgrading of Mile Cross Lane (as part of the new Ring Road) would open up the whole of that area between the two Lanes for industrial development. Norwich assembled and presented her case and a Local Government Commission was set up which, in 1963, proposed (amongst other things) the total elimination of Old Catton. The actual recommendation was that Old Catton, Hellesdon and Sprowston should all be absorbed by the city with Hellesdon and Sprowston becoming Wards, splitting Old Catton between them! This threat prompted a frenzy of fringe area meetings protesting at this high-handed action and Old Catton, at least, sent a strong letter to the Commission listing all the activities taking place in the parish, the Girl Guides, the British Legion, one of the first Women's Institutes, and all the other clubs and societies that made it such a lively village. In the event the fringe parishes won their case – or very nearly. The Minister's decision was to leave the city boundaries as they were with the exception of adding Bowthorpe in the west and, in the north, taking over the airfield and all the Old Catton land west of St Faiths Road. Further negotiations by the parish saved those roads adjacent to St Faiths Road on the western side, Louis Close, Taylors Lane and the top section of Fifers Lane. The Parish Council collectively breathed a sigh of relief at this settlement and it was only later that they realised that their budgetary provisions for street lighting, the Recreation Ground, etc had been calculated on the revenue from the industrial estate and the RAF housing now denied to them.

There have been other changes to the boundary through the years, the parameters have fluctuated back and forth, but nothing as drastic as the Norwich encroachment. In the early years of the century all houses on the western side of North Walsham Road were in Old Catton; later the boundary moved across the road to Moore Avenue, except for the George Hill area where, at one time, the proprietor of the grocer's shop on George Hill crossroads was in the peculiar position of having his shop in Old Catton and his bedroom in Sprowston! In January, 1992, the transfer of the Desmond Drive houses from Spixworth was approved after eight years of negotiations. Later, in 1998, an offer from Broadland District Council to simplify the parish boundary by moving it to the line of North Walsham Road was rejected by Sprowston Parish Council.

THE ROADS AND FOOTPATHS

In the late 1890s Catton had few roads. Spixworth Road led out of the city to Spixworth, Buxton and, ultimately, to Aylsham. North Walsham Road (or George Road as it was then known) came out of Norwich to Crostwick and Coltishall, and onwards, much as it does now, and had been a turnpike road for many years with a daily coach service between North Walsham and the City. St Faiths Road, over on the west side, joined Catton to Horsham St Faith by a route over Bullock Hill but from Fifers Lane to Catton Grove (the Low Road or Back Road as it was then called) it was merely a grass track and remained so until the early twenties. Lodge Lane was just a sandy track, whilst Taylors Lane was a farm road, cindered at the built-up end and then reverting to a grass track before leading through Mr Wharton's farmyard and on to Bullock Hill. The grass path from Taylors Lane across the meadow to Fifers Lane was part of an ancient track leading to St Augustines in Norwich but the ancient rights had lapsed and the farmer locked the farm gates at each side of the meadow once a year to signify that it was not a right of way. Taylors Lane was a right of way as was The Tills, another ancient path leading eastwards to North Walsham Road, and from that led another track to the farm at Dixons Fold.

The main centres of population in the village were still Church Street and George Hill but as the new century progressed, and more and more motor cars took to the roads, both George Hill and Oak Lane became part of an unofficial Northern Norwich Ring Road. A spate of accidents at the George Hill crossroads led to traffic lights being installed there around 1935, the first on the northern side of Norwich. World War II put a stop to this growth of motoring and it was not until the late 1940s that traffic began to thicken up once more and planners began turning their thoughts to improving our road layout.

Changes in the roads and paths of the village had been made necessary already by the building of the Airfield. Fifers Lane was widened and lost much of its hedges just prior to the war and was closed to civilian traffic throughout the war. When it re-opened it soon became a busy access road for the fast developing industrial estate centred around the new Vulcan Road and, from 1967 onwards, it began servicing the industrial estate created by Norwich City Council after they bought the airfield. St Faiths Road had been closed at Bullock Hill when the airfield was extended in 1943 to accommodate the American bombers and although several efforts were made to open an alternative link across the fields, St Faiths Road was permanently stopped at its junction with Quaker Lane by order of the Ministry of Transport in November, 1974. It was a tragedy, and somewhat ironic, that, having survived the demands and hazards of war, all thirteen new houses and bungalows which were built in 1936/7 along the northern section of St Faiths Road had to be demolished in 1955 to allow the main runway to be extended so that the new generation of jet fighters could use it. Ted Hawes lived in the last bungalow to be built there and for many years afterwards he was able to see the yellow daffodils from the bulbs that he and his father had planted in their garden. Taylors Lane, meanwhile, had been closed with a barbed wire fence in 1939, being designated a 'restricted place' by the Ministry of Defence, with access only for the residents of the cottages there and for tradesmen calling on them. It was re-opened briefly after the war, once more connecting up with Fifers Lane across the meadow but, in 1952, it was closed again to make the Air Ministry's section of the lane 'private'. The right of way along Taylors Lane to Bullock Hill had lapsed with the building of the airfield and the Parish Council could see little point in arguing over its status, particularly as the extended runways had severed this route to Horsham St Faith.

Meanwhile as time went on and the industrial estates grew, it was apparent that more needed to be done to Fifers Lane. An early suggestion was to build a link road from the old NAAFI shop round to the bend in the Back Road, thus diverting traffic away from the residential part of the Lane, and this was supported by the Parish Council but not by the City. The City Council subsequently gave their approval in 1970 but no definite steps were taken and in March, 1972, the County Council widened and re-aligned the junction of the Lane with St Faiths Road. The Parish Council campaigned again for the link road and one councillor, Mr Briscoe, made the prescient remark that "without the proposed link road it will become impossible for us to get out of Old Catton". The link road was never built, the County Council abandoning the idea for good in January, 1975, and the problems forecast by Mr Briscoe are with us still. It is possible that the Fiddlewood Estate, being planned by the City in 1974, was an overriding factor in their considerations but, whatever the reasons, this was one road which could have been but wasn't!

Another road which should have been but wasn't was the original Burma Road connection to Spixworth Road. This was clearly shown on the plans as being where the private road opposite Greyfriars now is whilst the road to the Post Office was to have been a cul-de-sac. The change was by mutual agreement between the builder, Mr Loveday, and the Rural District Council and created the existing awkward junction.

Spixworth Road itself was, in the early 1950s, the subject of much debate concerning the reinstatement of a Norwich to Cromer main road. The remnants of the original road (another turnpike) can still be seen – the south end is opposite The Firs public house, jutting incongruously into a patch of Hellesdon's now abandoned allotments and the north end emerges from the fields and into Horsham St Faith village. In January, 1955, it was proposed to use Spixworth Road to restore the link by way of Spixworth Church. The houses on the edge of the Burma Road development all had the building line set well back from the road in anticipation of a road-widening scheme but no decision was made until October, 1961, when it was decided to build an entirely new Cromer Road on the western edge of the airport.

The Norwich Ring Road was another project which was subject to prolonged discussion during the 1950s. It had been partially planned by the City Council prior to the war and already Sweetbriar Road and Boundary Road were in place, together with their two beacons to control the traffic. A Norwich planning map prepared in 1945 shows a proposed extension to this which would have utilised part of Fifers Lane and then gone across what is now Catton Chase and Woodland Drive and straight on to Sprowston. Needless to say this never got further than the drawing board. The eventual line involved the complete rebuilding of Mile Cross Lane and the building of an entirely new link to Wroxham Road. This was surveyed and planned in 1958 and finally built in 1963, much to the relief of the residents of Oak Lane, George Hill and School Lane. It was estimated that by this time at least 100 holiday coaches from Luton, Bedford and other Midland centres passed along these narrow lanes each Saturday during July and August taking holiday makers to and from the East Coast; it seems that Luton car factory employees were particularly fond of Caister and Hemsby as a venue for the August Bank Holiday.

The new ring road, however, produced its own crop of traffic problems at the open crossings of St Faiths Road and Spixworth Road and a spate of accidents at the latter junction led to rumours that Spixworth Road was to be closed. Suggestions for an underpass or a flyover were disregarded and the simpler remedy of erecting bollards to sever Spixworth Road from St Clements Hill was adopted in 1965. At the St Faiths Road junction the problem was solved by installing traffic lights so that city bound vehicles were assured of a safe passage across the ring road. But in the last quarter of the century Fifers Lane has become increasingly used as a short cut to the ring road by traffic coming down Cromer Road – such as the seasonal sugar beet lorries carting their loads from North Norfolk to Cantley – and, most recently, as the route adopted by the Airport Park and Ride buses. Constitution Hill, the third link between village and city, sought to overcome the ring road traffic by means of a large roundabout and this still impartially regulates the conflicting flows. But for how much longer? Mr Briscoe's warning could yet come true.

Near to Burma Road is our one and only right-of-way footpath, The Tills. This was a pleasant rural track before the war, passing through open fields at the top, past a woodland copse and then along the side of the Deer park, as it does today. In the early years of the century coffins were carried along this path on their way to burial at St Margaret's Church. Much of this rural charm was lost when Moore Avenue was developed and that part of the path enclosed with wooden fencing.

Finally the Village Green must be mentioned. At the turn of the century this was a triangle of grass at the top of Church Street upon which the first village sign was erected but with the increase of road traffic in the 1950s this became increasingly vulnerable and after a 'Keep Left' experiment in 1969 failed, the Green was expunged in October 1971.

26. Catton Hall Estate Laundry pictured in 1971 shortly before its demolition to enable the Garrick Green development to take place.

27. Flat-irons ready for use inside the laundry.

28. Another view of the old equipment inside the laundry.

29. Catton school in 1923, with pupil teacher Miss Rolph (later Mrs Liddington) on the left, and Miss Holmes on the right.

30. Catton School football team, 1934.   Noel Goff, Leslie Smith (goalkeeper), Reggie Morgan, Geoffrey Bringloe: Richard Lane, Ken Bullock, Bob Cushion, Albert Eke, Frank Betts, John Cooke, Jack Betts (Captain), Douglas Norgate, Jack Landamore, Ian Tokeley: John Seagrove, Reggie Smith.

31. Catton School dance team, 1935/6. Jack Landamore, Reg Smith, Reginald Morgan, Frank Betts, Geoffrey Bringloe, Leslie Potter, Avril White, Evelyn Symonds, Iris Youngman, Betty Giles, Irene Hall, Ivy Laws. *(Mrs I Whittaker)*.

32. Former headmaster Mr English addresses the crowd at the village Coronation Fete in 1953.

33. Blanche Pye, the long-serving teacher at Catton School *(A Pye).*

34. Trumpet Major Wix - licensee of the Woodman *(Courtesy The Woodman).*

35. Church Street, at the heart of the village, seen from the church tower in 1998 *(R Jon*es).

36. A 1905 postcard of Catton Hall showing the dome of the Camellia House still in place.

37. The gardens of Catton Hall looking north to the church in the 1930s, before the construction of Parkside Drive *(Courtesy A Buxton).*

38. A Doulton jug commissioned by the Buxton family to commemorate the coronation of Edward VII in 1902. Each household of Catton Hall Estate was presented with one by the Buxton family.

39. Old Catton Women's Institute and Parish Councillors at the junction of Woodland Drive and St Faiths Road in May 1966, following the presentation of a new seat to the village by the WI.

40. The Repton Pond at Parkside Drive with Catton Hall in the background. The site was acquired by Old Catton Society in 1994, and the picture illustrates the Millennium Railings project completed in 2000 *(R Jones)*.

41. The Busy Beavers playgroup pictured in 2000 - the future citizens of Old Catton *(R Jones)*.

SCHOOLS

For the first half of the century the formal education of the village children was solely in the hands of the teachers of the one existing school – Church Street School. Miss Alice Badcock was The Mistress and there were four other teachers on the staff of this Church of England Endowed School as the first term of 1900 got under way. Two of them, Blanche Pye and Louisa Holmes, were destined to stay with the school for the next thirty years or so, as was Miss M L Collin who joined as The Mistress in April, 1902; teaching was thus given a degree of stability and continuity to match the solidity of the school building itself.

By now the school was a well established feature of the village, having been built at the sole expense of Samuel Gurney Buxton (in the aftermath of Forster's Education Act of 1870) and was opened on the 5th of January, 1874, with Miss Georgiana Jackson as School Mistress. She was joined in March by Alice Harrowven and Emma Eastoe, described in the School Log Book as "candidate teachers", and was also assisted by Jane Hart, acting as school secretary, and Miss Millard who was not only the School Manager (a statutory post) but also voluntarily taught needlework to the girls.

Not all the children were enthusiastic about this new opportunity for widening their horizons and Sheila Currall remembers the family story of how her grandfather (Jack Badcock, the blacksmith's son) and his friends, spent their playtimes at the new school by picking at the mortar of the walls in the hope that it would fall down! But the school remained standing and at the end of the first year Her Majesty's Inspector reported "A good beginning of work has been made in this school" and then, alarmed that this might be too laudatory, added "The spelling is somewhat weak". The school was now on a firm footing with an adequate supply of pens, composition books and arithmetic cards, and an average attendance approaching the 100 mark; that is apart from the occasional days in October when children and their parents gave priority to acorn gathering for their pigs. The catchment area for these children stretched from Rackham Fields (near Philadelphia Lane) and the cottages at the far end of Mile Cross Lane in one direction and Spixworth village in the other. The boundary change in 1907 led to the eventual departure of the 'Fields' children and the growth of Catton Grove and the opening of a new school there accelerated this process but the Spixworth children continued to attend Catton school for many more years. In those days there was no alternative to walking so it is not surprising that attendance slackened during periods of bad weather. In February, 1904, the School Log records that four boys were absent because of "the want of boots".

The old school building still stands in Church Street but in the early years of the century it seemed much more prominent being situated on the other side of the pond from the smithy and looking out over Catton Hall park to the front and the expanse of the stack yard and Butter Close behind. It consisted of the main, central room (50ft by 18ft) flanked on the eastern side by the infants room (20ft by 18ft) and on the western side by the room designated as the Village Reading Room, which in practice was 'borrowed' from time to time for overflow classes. The building was austere looking on the outside, spartan inside. The rooms were lit by gas mantles, hanging on long chains from the rafters (no ceilings here!) and operated by a pole and hook; they had recently replaced oil lamps which themselves had superseded candles. The floor was of wooden blocks laid on bare earth and loose enough to be lifted in order to retrieve pencils and drawing pins lost down the cracks. Heating was by open coal fires which warmed the teacher but not much else. Outside, the girls' toilets, or closets as they were known, consisted of a brick and timber structure equipped with buckets, whilst the boys' 'offices' was an open-air drain; the playground, encompassed by the brick wall was of hard earth with many an embedded stone for tripping on. It was in the playground that four Lime trees were planted (with the aid of selected boys) to commemorate Edward VII's coronation in 1902. The standard of teaching, however, must have been more than adequate for, in 1910, Elsie Cracknell became the first child in the school to win a County Council Scholarship – to the Higher Grade School in Norwich. Her photograph was displayed in the school for some years afterwards, perhaps as pride in her achievement, perhaps as a spur to greater efforts!

The outbreak of war in 1914 was hardly noticed by the school as it took place during the Harvest Holidays but its effects were soon felt as fathers and older brothers left home to enlist. The more sombre side of war made its impact on the village in September, 1915, when Catton Hospital opened up in the Hall museum; it catered for convalescent soldiers and they were soon talking to and befriending the children. Tragedy struck the school in October when Miss Woolnough was absent for several days to mourn her father who had been killed in Flanders on the 26th September; in July and August, 1916, overnight Zeppelin raids reduced attendances at the school. But the main disruptions to the everyday teaching were caused by outbreaks of scarlet fever, measles and the like, and an influenza epidemic in the winter of 1916 took its toll of the teachers as well as the pupils. The normal routine at this time was also disrupted by the introduction of a 10am start for the school, this came into force on the 3rd of November, 1916, and was to last throughout the winter months – no doubt a remedy for the darker mornings created by the newly introduced British Summer Time.

In the 1920s there was still only a very gradual change in the physical look of the school building. By now there was a gas stove in the reading room for the girls' cookery classes and in 1929 teaching was made easier by the addition of a permanent screen in place of the rudimentary curtain that subdivided the main room; henceforth each of the two classes had its own room instead of just sitting back-to-back as previously. They sat in pairs, each pair sharing a bench and a desk, beneath which was a shelf for books and personal possessions and there were two china inkwells on each desk which the monitors were allowed to fill. The ink was made by chosen boys who mixed up the powder and water in the sink of the cloakroom. The heating was still by open fire, now surrounded by a fire-guard, and Sheila Currall remembers that the children were allowed to put their bottles of milk by the fire to warm up during the winter ("a kind of rice pudding skin formed on the top!"). Each school day started with a hymn and prayers and the first lesson was always Religious Education – the New Testament one day, the Old Testament on another day, main church services on another and the Catechism on yet another. It was, after all, a church school and the children were inspected annually for Religious Instruction. The rest of the morning was spent on the three Rs, History and Geography, but the afternoons often included arts and crafts and senior girls were instructed in the art of cookery on that single gas stove in the Reading Room – cakes, buns and biscuits were the product.

The teaching staff, however, was subject to some radical changes during this period. Miss Collin retired on the 30th September, 1921, after 19 years service and, sadly, Miss Holmes, the infants teacher, died on the 30th November, 1931, after nearly 39 years at the school. Moreover the retirement of Miss Collin opened the way for the first male teacher at the school. This was the Revd G S Taylor and, although he lasted no more than six months, he was succeeded by Mr Jack Bishop who stayed for six years and successfully guided two children, Doris Gallant and Fred Bensley, to scholarship awards in 1926. He also started a National Savings scheme for the school and, at the suggestion of the School Inspector in 1927, arranged for senior boys and girls to go to Heather Avenue school in Hellesdon once a week for woodwork and cookery. The same Inspector reported that "the last three years have been a period of steady progress and the school as a whole is now in a very satisfactory condition". A different perspective obtained from the school room floor, however, because John Lane remembers Mr Bishop as "a nice little man who was not able to keep order and we did as we liked when he was there."

The satisfactory condition was to be further improved and the educational spectrum considerably enhanced and widened when, in May, 1928, Mr English, a certificated teacher trained at college, arrived to take over the school. He brought with him a much wider view of education than any of his predecessors. Art was one of his strengths as was sport and athletics. He started competitive football for the boys and, in June, 1932, had a concrete strip laid in the playground for cricket practice. He appropriated Church Street as a school running track and *Frank Betts* remembers "training for the school sports – 100 yards was from Spixworth Road to the school gate, 220 yards from The Maids Head to the school gate and the 440 yards from school gate to The Maids Head and back; the teachers stood at each end to direct what traffic might come along". Mr English was also eager to instil into his pupils an appreciation of music (he was himself a member of the Norwich Amateur Operatic Society) and to this end he would notate the morning hymn on the blackboard to encourage the children to read music. More entertainingly from their point of view, he supplemented this by inviting local amateur musicians to perform for the school. Thus an entry in the School Log for 30th of June, 1929, reads: "A useful lesson in musical appreciation was given to the children this afternoon by Mrs Tillett whose string Quartet visited the school". Mrs Tillett was the former Marriette Carter of The Elms and the Quartet was completed by her two sisters, Adeline and Renee, and her brother, Oscar. These efforts of Mr English were well rewarded as the school went on to take part in the County Schools Annual Music Festival held in St Andrews Hall, Norwich.

But the credit is not solely his as he was superbly supported by Miss Blanche Pye. She had begun her teaching career at the school as a Monitress in 1896 and, early on, had sought to take the children beyond the three Rs – in 1910, the School Log Book refers to her taking pupils for nature walks, whilst her butterfly collection was a cause of wonderment amongst the children. Maire Booty remembers classes being taken into the woods on the Hellesdon side of the Back Road with lists of things to find – "We once found a wild bees' nest abandoned in the hedge; the boys dug it out and we took it back to the school and rebuilt it". It was the arrival of Mr English that really allowed Miss Pye's talents in teaching needlework, nature study and country dancing to blossom. It was she who made sure that the school participants in the St Andrews Hall Festival were dressed smartly, even to the extent of buying navy blue trousers for the boys whose parents could not afford them. Each year the school entered the competition and in 1939 they won the County Shield for Country Dancing. Blanche Pye was now in her middle years and, with her gold-framed glasses half way down her nose, she dispensed a motherly influence over her pupils. William Kelter remembers that it was something of a shock when the time came to move up to Mr English's class, with his rule of iron exercised by a bent cane!

Together, the energetic, disciplinarian Mr English and the kindly, caring Miss Pye moulded the school for more than twenty years and were loyally supported by a third long-serving teacher, Miss Ethel Woolnough. She began as an Assistant Mistress in May, 1912, and for many years taught Standards I and II at the school, as well as conducting a clothing savings scheme for the poorer children. The class structure of the various Standards was, incidentally, materially altered when Sprowston Secondary Modern School opened in 1938 and Catton lost its 12+ age group, and the school register dropped from over 100 to 85. Miss Woolnough transferred to Sprowston Junior school and was replaced on 21st February, 1938, by Miss Kathleen Matthews. Interestingly, when the new Sprowston school first opened the eligible children living in Old Catton were issued, not with bus passes, but with new bicycles and yellow oilskins – much to the envy of those who had passed 'The Scholarship' and received only bus passes to get them to the Norwich grammar schools! Outside the school, one unwelcome, but not to be ignored, visitor was the school dentist; he came twice a year and parked his van beside the pond, bringing fear to the children at the thought of his foot-pedal operated drill.

Greater disruption occurred in September, 1939, when the outbreak of another war caused the opening of the Autumn term to be delayed until the 11th September and even then only 68 children attended out of a total roll call of 110 (including one evacuee). This was, perhaps, a protest against the fact that no air raid shelters had been provided for the school. In the event, these were not completed until the end of March, 1940, and were not used 'for real' until the 9th of July, 1940, when the first air raid warning during school hours was sounded. It was the first of many such visits to the shelters during that summer and winter but it was not until the Norwich 'Blitz' that the School Log recorded, on the 28th April, 1942, that many children were absent because of "severe aerial bombardment" and that Miss Middleton was absent because her lodgings had been damaged.

Otherwise, school routines went on much as usual, enlivened only by the occasional air raid drill and gas mask inspection. One novelty was the arrival of an American officer on the 26th November, 1942, to give the children a talk about Thanksgiving Day, a feature that was repeated in subsequent years. The end of the war in Europe was marked by two days holiday and when they returned on the 10th May it was to find that the school Union Jack had been cut from the flag pole overnight. Perhaps another souvenir destined to cross the 'Big Pond'?

In the first few years following the war there were staff upheavals in schools throughout the country as teachers returned from the forces and allowed their elderly colleagues to enter into, or return to, retirement. At Church Street School Miss Blanche Pye retired on the 19th March, 1948, and Mr Bill English followed her into well earned retirement in December of that year. He was replaced by Mr Geoffrey H Deller who began his own long service to the school and became, incidentally, the first school head not to live in the village, whilst Mrs Baker, who had been a pupil teacher in the 1920s returned for a while as a senior mistress. At this time, too, student teachers were coming to the school for brief practical experience as the final part of their course under an Emergency Teacher

Training Scheme being conducted at Keswick Hall Training College. Miss Downing arrived for a five week stint in 1951 and found she had to instruct a class of forty 7-9 year olds; even more daunting was the discovery that there was no staff room and so, perforce, for every PT lesson she had to change into her blouse and shorts in the class room – shielded only by the blackboard and easel! One at least of the pre-war teachers remained and that was Miss Kathleen Matthews who had started at the school in 1938 and did not retire until 1974, by which time the school around her had changed out of all recognition.

In the meantime, however, Mr Deller had to contend with things as they were and this included coping with the gas lighting. The gas mantles tended to explode when they were ignited on winter's afternoons and he always instructed the children to cover their faces by pressing into the desk tops before he proceeded. But change was coming. In July, 1949, control of the school passed to the Norfolk Education Committee and it became a Voluntary Controlled school. It had started in the 19th Century as a Church of England Endowed school and later became a Voluntary Aided school and now it was entirely funded by the local education authority. The first visible result flowing from this move was the removal of the wood block floor in 1954 and, by 1961, the school not only had a plastic tiled floor but also electricity, flush toilets, wash basins, water heaters, two slow combustion stoves and, progress indeed, a telephone! Despite the loosening of the ties with St Margaret's Church, however, the Vicar, the Revd Darbyshire-Bowles, continued to teach RI at the school every Tuesday and Thursday and a Diocesan representative examined the children on their religious knowledge once a year. These procedures lapsed after the Vicar retired but for some years the whole school, as an organised body, continued to attend church twice a year (on Ash Wednesday and Ascension Day), with the parents being given the option of withdrawing their children if they wished. Even when that lapsed, a Christmas Carol Service, involving the whole school, was performed in St Margaret's each year until well into the 70s.

The school register also was not immune from this general climate of change. Having been reduced by the opening of the new Sprowston Secondary Modern school in 1938, the post war period now saw a marked increase in numbers attending the school. There was a national baby boom in the late forties and this was supplemented by the gradual development of housing in Old Catton and Spixworth and by the fully occupied Airmen's Married Quarters in Fifers Lane. By 1954 the school was overcrowded and the Norfolk Education Authority sought to remedy this by appropriating two huts on Fifers Lane, near to the Vicarage, as an infant class for the RAF children. This was not only physically inconvenient for the teachers but imposed additional organisational problems and, in any case, the Old Catton Parish Council insisted that "they are village children and deserve to be educated with the rest of our parishioners".

Nevertheless by the spring of 1955 these two huts were catering for 55 children up to the age of 8 and there was a total school register of 217 – the Parish Hall was being used as a classroom as well as the school dining room (a function it had been fulfilling since 1947). The Church Street building was patently no longer big enough or equipped sufficiently well for post war children and the Norfolk Education Authority was pressed to find a suitable site for a new school. They considered the field alongside The Beeches at the bottom of George Hill and Currie's Meadow at the back of Catton Court (this site eventually became the infants school in Garrick Green) but were finally persuaded by the Parish Council to build on Butter Close next to the old school. A start was made on two new classrooms in 1955, "to form the basis of a new school", and by 1958 they were ready for occupation. The following year plans were laid for a new assembly hall and kitchen and, in 1963, three more classrooms were added. The school was completed in 1966 when a headmaster's study and a secretary's office were attached. But the numbers of children attending continued to rise and it was considered prudent to keep the old building in use, particularly as it now had the additional benefit of central heating. The school, though, was happy to relinquish its grasp on the huts and the Village Hall.

It did not take long for Mr Deller to establish his authority and personality on the school. Unlike Bill English he did not favour the cane and used it only once, and then it was sufficient to scare the miscreant boy by bringing it down hard on the desk! Academically he was quietly pleased when he brought five pupils through the 11+ at his first attempt and so beat Bill English's best effort of four. The accent on out of school activities was also enthusiastically continued. The school took part in Country Dance meetings at the Sprowston Recreation Ground school, along with teams from Spixworth and Horsham St Faith schools and, later, Catton school was selected to give a display of such dancing at the Royal Norfolk Show. Mr Deller was also one of the first to organise school day trips out of the county and took several coach parties to London for the usual sights and, on one occasion, to be shown around Parliament by Brigadier Medlicott, the local MP. And, of course, the school football team continued to be very active, although without a pitch of its own in those early post-war years; they practised on the grassy area by the stack-yard and turned up on Saturday mornings to cycle to wherever the day's match was to be played.

After 1966 the whole character of the school began to change. Enlarged and modernised, it started to edge away from its village school image and to take on, gradually, the status of a Middle School (its new designation in 1977). New teachers began to fill the new classrooms and Mr Deller gained the inestimable support of a Deputy Head, in the shape of Mr Hickling. Fred Hickling had progressed through one of the new training colleges after leaving HM forces and had obtained teaching experience elsewhere before arriving at Church Street school where his sturdy common sense and warm personality had a great influence. All aspiring teachers were now being properly trained, unlike earlier days of the century when certificated teachers were in the minority and able exponents of the art, such as Blanche Pye and Kathleen Matthews, were unqualified and had learnt the job as they taught their charges. Miss Matthews, in fact, was away on a year's teaching course when Mr Deller first arrived at the school.

Another teacher who joined shortly after the completion of the expansion scheme was Mary Manning. She had already spent several years teaching at North Walsham and in Norwich and now faced up to fresh challenges – for one school year she had 52 children in her class. This was not necessarily an insuperable problem as the Old Catton children responded to good teaching and, in one particularly good year in the 70s, a record total of 25 of them passed the 11+ exam (completely shattering Geoffrey Deller's earlier record). Mary Manning was instrumental in expanding on Mr Deller's day trips when she persuaded the Norfolk Education Committee to sanction week long educational field trips. This was the first time such a scheme had been undertaken by any Middle School in Norfolk and there followed a succession of annual adventures to such places as the Isle of Wight and Derbyshire. These expeditions were not entered into in any carefree fashion and it soon became the rule that they should be preceded by practice walks to Mousehold and back which tested not only young muscles but new boots! In addition, the lessons for some months earlier were, in part, focussed on the intended field trip area so that its history, geology, geography, wild life and industry could be anticipated; one group was quite impressed to see the actual diaries of the Bronte sisters (in the Bronte museum) after being told about them in earlier school lessons.

It was also during the 1970s that the school was able to take advantage of the playing fields that came with the new school buildings; sporting activities were extended to include netball and basketball, whilst the cricket and athletic teams now had the luxury of properly laid out pitches and tracks. In an unwitting evocation of the spirit of Blanche Pye, Mary Manning (with the assistance of parents) turned her hand to the making of tunics for the netball team. She recalls that despite the deliberately large hems on these tunics they were still not big enough for succeeding classes – a situation she ascribes to the rapid increase in average height of girls during the 1970s!

By 1970 there were 398 children attending the school (compared with the pre-war average of approximately 100) and the Education Authority took the radical decision to build more schools in the village. Old Catton was now changing its shape. There were large housing projects in the pipe line (or, indeed, actually built) all over the northern edge of the village and this was the obvious area to position new schools. White Woman Lane school was opened in September,

1971, to supply the needs of the Proctor Road area (and in reality is just over the border into Sprowston). It was intended as an infant and junior school, relieving Church Street of 60 of its pupils, but became a Middle school in 1978 at the same time as Church Street achieved this status. Infant schools at Lodge Lane and Garrick Green were opened in 1976 and 1977 respectively and the overcrowding problem was, for the time being, solved. Even the flow of children from the Fiddlewood Estate (officially part of Norwich) has failed to put pressure on accommodation and, in fact, in 1984 Mr Jackson, Church Street's present Headmaster, reported that of the 235 pupils at Church Street only 45% came from the village itself, 35% came from Fiddlewood, 12% from RAF quarters and 8% from the Sprowston and Norwich fringes, and that "without these out-of-parish children the school would not be viable and would probably be closed".

It had been the aim of the Norfolk Education Committee to close down the old school once the new buildings were in full operation and to offer it to the Parish Council for general use. This intention had been conveyed to the Parish Council in 1955 and again in 1971 but on each occasion the statement was followed by a fresh outbreak of house building and an increase in the school register so that the old school could not be released from its original task. Is it destined to remain a school always or will it, one day, become an additional social centre for the village and revive memories of the old Victorian Reading Room?

CATTON HALL

For the first half of the century the village was dominated by Catton Hall. This unpretentious but comfortable mansion was built in 1780, just before the French Revolution, and occupied an imposing site on the crest of a hill which sloped gently down to Catton Grove, giving its occupants a fine view of distant Norwich. This view was improved further when the owner gave Humphry Repton his first commission to create a landscaped parkland now, alas, sadly deteriorated by age and human interference. The house itself was considerably enhanced when John Henry Gurney added the wrought iron Camellia House in the 1850s. He did this possibly in emulation of Joseph Caxton's great glass and iron edifice at the Great Exhibition of 1851 and employed the local architect, Edward Boardman, to design it and the expanding Norwich firm of Boulton and Paul to construct it. Mr Gurney also made other improvements to the house (a new ballroom and bay windows) and built the terrace of cottages in Church Street for the estate workers. The Hall reached its zenith, however, during its ownership by Samuel Gurney Buxton (1866 to 1909). He was a prominent member of the Norwich Liberal Party and during his mayoralty in 1873–1874 he organised a considerable number of civic celebrations where Catton Hall was often the venue for important receptions. In August, 1883, after formally opening the new Norfolk and Norwich Hospital, the Duke and Duchess of Connaught and Prince Albert stayed overnight at the Hall as guests of Sam Buxton, and no doubt strolled around the ornately laid out gardens on the north side of the house the next morning. Other celebrities also savoured the tranquillity of these quiet gardens, the rockeries, the water gardens and ordered flower beds; one for instance was the cricketer, W G Grace, who stayed overnight when playing at Lakenham cricket ground during the summer of 1903. The preceding year Mr Buxton celebrated the Coronation of Edward VII by presenting each of his estate workers with a specially commissioned Doulton jug bearing the motif of the cat and of the barrel. Several of these 'Catton Jugs', brown with white embellishments, still survive in the village today.

By the turn of the century the park-land had been thickened along its western side by a Victorian woodland fringe of conifers, sprinkled with majestic Wellingtonias, and between the ornamental gardens and the Georgian Orangery (then a well filled museum of stuffed birds and animals) had grown up a collection of green houses wherein the gardeners, 15 in number, successfully grew grapes, figs, peaches, melons and nectarines as well as the more conventional crops of tomatoes, cucumbers and mushrooms. The gardeners were also responsible for the cricket ground on the eastern side of the house, two tennis courts and a bowling green, and the kitchen gardens and orchards to the north of Church Street. There was no lack of employment!

Inevitably the maintenance of this house and its estate – which included the Fiddle Wood, arable fields stretching half way up the south side of Fifers Lane, and the kitchen gardens, hay meadow and orchards to the north of Church Street – required many workers. The footman lived in the cottages alongside the drive, known as The Bothy, and the head gardener lived in the cottage on the right of the drive gates (the cottage on the left was reserved for the school mistress). The cottages in Church Street were occupied by gardeners, domestics, the gamekeeper and the wood forester and there were still more estate cottages in Spixworth Road; the saddler and the blacksmith lived and had their work-places in Church Street, and the laundress was appropriately installed way back by the laundry. The Church Street cottages, incidentally, all had neatly trimmed box hedging, tracing different patterns, in their front gardens (like individual knot gardens) and they were required to grow in these gardens the flowers and bulbs given to them each year by Mr Edward Gurney Buxton, who became the new owner of Catton Hall in 1909 on the death of his father. Older villagers remember the red geraniums and blue lobelia as being particularly colourful. These cottage gardens formed part of the attractions for Sunday walkers from Norwich as they strolled around the periphery of the parkland and through the well tended woods of Oak Lane and the Back Road. The wooded areas outside the park have gone and the parkland itself is looking more desolate – not least because a sizeable part of it had to be ploughed up during the war for essential food production - but a few of the box hedge gardens remain. Another attraction for the Sunday strollers would have been the deer in the Deer Park (that solitary piece of the park that exists on the eastern side of Spixworth Road). Deer were introduced by Samuel Gurney Buxton before the end of the 19th Century and remained there until the severe winter of 1926 killed them off.

This idyllic scene was rudely, but temporarily, shattered by the Great War of 1914−18 when not only was the male population decimated by enrolment but the Racquets Court and the Museum were, in 1915, converted into Catton Hall VAD Hospital for convalescent soldiers. Social occasions were replaced by the task of caring for these wounded men and Edward Buxton's wife, Laura, rose to the challenge by taking charge of the general administration of the hospital, whilst her husband supplied (sometimes surreptitiously) beer and cigarettes to the men. The parkland and gardens were then mainly appreciated by the convalescents, whilst the Hall kitchen was often called upon to supplement the hospital's more primitive wooden, lean-to kitchen.

But the war ended and in February, 1919, the remaining convalescents were dispersed, the hospital closed down and Mrs Buxton was awarded the MBE by a grateful government. Slowly the estate reverted to its pre-war way of life with, however, a single but significant exception. In September of that year Edward Buxton offered the use of the museum and its attached wartime kitchen to the Parish Council for use as a Parish Hall. The building was legally transferred by him to two of the Parish Councillors, Alfred Finch and Henry Carter, at a nominal rent of 1/- per annum (including the use of the 'glory hole' coal store, the furniture and the piano!) and henceforward village organisations had a properly managed meeting place for all their activities. The building became even more vital to village life as the old Reading Room attached to the school was gradually absorbed for use as another classroom. Somewhat incongruously it still held all the trappings of its former life as a museum; wildlife display cases lined the walls, containing the trophies of Samuel Buxton's travels both at home and abroad and a magnificent stag's head hung above the large open fireplace. Unfortunately there were no toilets and nature's needs were catered for by two earth closets situated amongst the trees outside.

The gardeners returning from the war were reinforced by Captain Buxton's wartime batman, to whom he offered employment on the estate, and by young lads as they left the Church Street school. John Bunting, one of the young lads, actually started working here in 1929, straight from school, but undoubtedly his memories are an accurate record of the gardens as they must have been just ten years earlier. He recalls not only the exotic greenhouses but also the cold frames where pot plants were brought on; violets were especially popular, such as the single Princess of Wales and the Marie Louisa double, whilst another favourite was the Lorraine begonia. As he grew more experienced he was charged with watering the potted plants in the various rooms of the Hall, the morning room, the smoking room, the hallway, etc, and even the wrought iron conservatory which, at that time, had five large camellias and a Marshall Neil rose which was running rampant along the back wall. The cricket pitch and bowling green were brought back into full use and it was also necessary to ensure that the hay was harvested and carted off from the cricket ground area.

An important part of the Catton Estate was the Hall Farm on Church Street which had been redesigned and modernised by John Henry Gurney so that the stables were grouped around the yards. The Holmes family moved into this farm in 1927. Mr Holmes had been employed by Sir Eustace Gurney at Sprowston Hall but felt unable to follow Sir Eustace when the latter moved to Walsingham Abbey and so Sir Eustace arranged for him to be engaged at Catton Hall farm. This was a dairy farm with cream cheese and butter being made on the premises and, quite apart from the usual milk rounds, there was a steady demand for milk from the children in the school opposite; the children could hardly be unaware of the farm as, during the summer, the cow herd was turned out to graze on the pasture behind the school. Mr Holmes's son Walter, looked after the horses on the estate, mostly cart horses but also some 'fast' horses for the gigs and traps.

Then, in April, 1929, Mr Edward Buxton died. He had been the 'pater familias' of the estate and of the village since 1909, when his father died, and although he became Mayor of Norwich in 1907 he always saw himself as more of a business man than a politician and immersed himself in the banking activities of Barclays of Bank Plain; the daily journey to the city in his gig was a feature of Old Catton life. One of his first acts after becoming the new owner of Catton Hall was to open, in July, 1909, Sewell Park at the foot of St Clements Hill, after already financing the construction of it. As already mentioned in 1919 he provided the Parish Hall for the village and in 1921 he gave a small piece of the Deer Park as a site for Old Catton's War Memorial.

His son, Desmond, now abandoned his career in the army and returned from India to take charge of the estate. Whether his new status as head of the family accelerated his courtship of Rachel Morse we know not but certainly, in January 1930, the two of them were married. This may have been the last occasion on which the family coach was used. Certainly times were changing for Catton Hall, as they were for the rest of the world. The Wall Street crash and the resulting world-wide depression obliterated the optimism of the 20s. Unemployment in England rose rapidly to more than two million and Old Catton was not immune. The number of gardeners on the estate was reduced from fifteen to ten. The two chauffeurs were discharged and Walter Holmes was told to attend Mann Egertons in Norwich to learn to drive so that he could combine his equine duties with the mechanical.

Some aspects of life, however, continued unchanged at the Hall. In May, 1937, Mrs Rachel Buxton, together with the Vicar's wife, Mrs McCready, presented a Coronation Mug and a New Testament to each of the children at Church Street school, thus continuing the tradition established by Mrs Laura Buxton when she presented Coronation goblets to the children in 1911. At the start of each summer the hay was harvested from the expansive grassy area in front of the Hall in readiness for the cricket season and for the Sunday School treats and the Summer Fetes. The Sunday School Outings for Norwich children at Catton Hall were an established tradition and on the appointed day the scrubbed and decorated coal carts, filled with excited children, would turn into the park by the gateway alongside The Maids Head row of cottages; thereafter the day would be filled with games, dancing, gymnastic displays and, of course, the anticipated special tea, and after a rousing chorus of "For he's a jolly good fellow" the children would depart. The Summer Fetes were also a feature of life at Catton Hall and we are fortunate to have a contemporary account of one of these provided by the W.I. notes in the parish magazine of August, 1932. It reads as follows:-

"On Thursday, July 21st, the proposed Garden Fete in aid of the Queen's Purse Fund was held in the delightful grounds of Catton Hall, kindly

placed at the disposal of the Old Catton Women's Institute by Capt. D G and Mrs Buxton. Mrs Woolsey, who presided, welcomed Mrs Alfred Finch, formerly President before removing to East Tuddenham. Mrs Finch, in declaring the Fete open, gave a brief outline of the objects of the Queen's Purse Fund, and said she felt sure that Old Catton would do its share towards it. The weather was glorious and tastefully arranged stalls were soon doing a brisk business. These consisted of Pound Stall, Work Stall, Flowers and Produce, White Elephant, and Refreshments; the Wishing Well, prettily decorated, was a great attraction to the children. The Side Shows included Hoop-la, Coconut Shies, Ring Bowls, Treasure Hunt, etc. A cricket match was arranged by Capt. Buxton between Barclay's Bank and the Norfolk County Council, which resulted in a win for the latter. During the interval for tea the players also patronised the Side Shows. Teas were served on the Rink by the Tea Committee and their helpers. An open air Whist Drive took place in the evening, twenty hands being played. The Stop Watch was won by Art Morgan. As a result of our efforts the sum of £25 has been handed over as the Old Catton Women's Institute contribution towards the Queen's Purse Fund."

One of the main leisure pursuits of the gentry was shooting and partridge shoots around Old Catton were just as popular as ever, being facilitated by the estate gamekeeper, Billy Harrowven (at a later date Fred Church took over). Walter Holmes remembers using a horse and trap to take guns, cartridges and lunch out to a shoot at Felthorpe. His task was to stand by the trap ready to hand out additional cartridges and then, at about 4pm, he would collect the dead birds and take them to the gamekeeper's cottage for counting. He recalls that Mr Buxton always gave him a shot hare at the start of each season.

Then, incredibly, the world was caught up in another great war and Captain Buxton left the Hall to take command of a territorial battalion of the Royal Norfolk Regiment. Some months later Catton Hall was requisitioned by the army and Mrs Buxton and her three children perforce had to leave, first taking up residence in a hurriedly rented house in Coltishall, then to Scotland and Warwickshire in a vain attempt to keep in touch with her husband, and finally to Heggatt Hall. Most of the other gentry had also moved away from Old Catton as the proximity of the aerodrome, opened in 1939, made the village a potentially dangerous place. In the event, only 30 bombs (plus a lot of incendiaries) were dropped on the village, several on the Hall parkland, and only little damage was done. One of the early defensive measures was to remove the dome of the Camellia House as it was feared that it made a good landmark – probably reflecting the moonlight on its convex surface.

As with other empty houses the army was quick to move into Catton Hall and in 1940 the parkland was dotted with the tents of a territorial artillery regiment.

They were followed in 1942 by a battalion of Gordon Highlanders and in consequence the frontage of the Hall frequently resounded to the martial airs of a Highland Pipe Band as they marched and counter-marched before their officers who, of course, were billeted in the Hall. Towards the end of 1942 the Hall and its environs became occupied by a signals unit of the 76th Training Division. The top floor of the Hall became a dormitory for troops, whilst the ground and first floors of the Hall were used as offices for the ATS clerks and administrative staff. And yet some semblance of pre-war life remained as Betty Davis, one of those military clerks, remembers the picturesque gardens and also remembers fetes (but these were 'Battle for Britain' fetes) taking place each summer in front of the Hall; normality to the extent that one fete featured the loudspeakers booming out "We're having a heat wave" as the rain tippled down! The Parish Hall was turned into a NAAFI and all the stuffed animals were thrown out but its loss of use for the village was made good, to some extent, when the army allowed the Racquets Court to be used for social occasions.

By the war's end Catton Hall was showing the signs of its extended military occupation and although the Buxton family returned to the house in 1946, Desmond Buxton quickly realised that six years of army use had left it entirely unfit for bringing up a family and, after six months or so of careful deliberation, he arranged to buy Hoveton Hall. The Buxton residency of Catton Hall had come to an end. It was not until 1948, however, that a willing purchaser, in the shape of Norfolk County Council, materialised for the empty property and in August of that year the Hall and 27 acres of land surrounding it passed into the public domain for a purchase figure of £8000. It was then converted into an Old People's Home. Ten years later, Mr Buxton offered outright ownership of the Parish Hall, plus the skating rink and the approach via the stable yard, to the village, and formally handed over the keys in a brief ceremony on the 13th December, 1960. The post-war demand for new homes encouraged Mr Buxton to continue selling off parts of the estate lands as has been described earlier and, more importantly for the village as a whole, the old Butter Close was sold to the Parish Council to become a recreation ground for the village. The community benefited again in 1973 when the old smithy and land behind the school and the Church Street cottages were sold off for housing and sufficient land was set aside there for the building of a Church Hall; Desmond Buxton also donated £1000 towards the building of it. In 1984 the old Hall Farm in Church Street was converted into housing and, as the century drew to a close, planning application was made to build on one of the last remaining fragments of the estate – twelve large houses on the abandoned allotments off Fifers Lane (the very same allotments that had been moved in 1957).

In the meantime Norfolk County Council, in 1985, had sought to demolish the Camellia House because of the costs of maintenance but had been thwarted by public opposition (not least from the newly formed Old Catton Society) and the wrought iron structure remains. The Council, however, found it increasingly difficult to operate the Hall as an old people's home and the residents were moved to other accommodation in 1990. Failing to find any other suitable use for the building (although it provided very acceptable temporary accommodation for staff and pupils when Hall School was badly damaged by fire in November 1993), the Council put it up for sale in 1994. The asking price was £350,000 and a year or so later it was bought by Mr and Mrs Mike and Patsy Cooke as a home and as offices for his business, Wensum Insurance Agency, a business he had set up after his career in the RAF was brought to an end by a flying accident during an aerobatic display. The ballroom was converted into an open plan office for up to 20 staff and there was still enough space left in the commodious old Hall for the creation of half dozen or so spacious flats.

The sale left just one fragment of the old Edwardian splendours – the ornamental pond, with its fountain, that had formed the centrepiece of the Hall's formal gardens. It had already become isolated from Catton Hall by the creation and development of Parkside Drive and it formed no part of the sale of the Hall in 1994. The County Council regarded it as an anachronistic encumbrance and was anxious to dispose of it. When it became apparent that the Parish Council was disinclined to take it over the Old Catton Society, with some misgivings, made enquiries and found itself becoming a property owner at a nominal cost of £5. Since then the members of the Society have spent much energy in upgrading this quiet corner, and pursued a Millennium project that has enclosed the pond with fine new iron railings.

Not all the planned developments were approved over the years. A major proposal in 1990, that the remaining expanse of park land rolling down from the Hall to Oak Lane and the Ring Road should be surrendered to the control of Broadland District Council so that it could be opened up as a general public amenity, was rejected after a good deal of controversy. The plan foundered on the hotly contested scheme to build thirty three houses on the top end of the Deer Park which was an integral part of the whole project and was intended to provide funds to help restore and maintain the Park. So, as the century ends, Old Catton still awaits its opportunity to inherit Humphry Repton's parkland.

THE CHURCH

At the heart of the village, figuratively if not literally, is St Margaret's Church. It has been there, stolidly, since at least the 14th Century but it was during the period 1850–1861 that it underwent a considerable transformation. The South Aisle and the double North Transept were added and new pews installed, together with a 16th Century pulpit which had been removed from St George's Church in Colegate, Norwich. These works were all due to the energy and enthusiasm of the incumbent at that time, the Revd Richard Hart, allied to the monetary support of the then owners of Catton Hall, George Morse and then John Henry Gurney, and were in accord with the prevailing Victorian desire to update their places of worship. When the 20th Century began, therefore, St Margaret's was in good order and little more needed doing over the subsequent years. Even today the building, from the outside, looks much as it did then, except that the ivy has been cleared from the walls.

Similarly, the extent of its parish has not changed much over the century. It still stretches westwards for half the length of Fifers Lane and eastwards to the line of Constitution Hill and Moore Avenue; in the south, it has contracted back to the line of the Ring road, and in the north east corner it has expanded to embrace the Desmond Drive area that had been transferred to the civil parish in 1992. But this is only in the terms of area. The once open fields on the western side of the village have now filled with homes (to the south of Fifers Lane) and a bustling industrial estate (on the north side of Fifers Lane). Moreover, the great majority of these homes, those in Fiddlewood, are within the city boundary so that St Margaret's is in the unusual position of ministering to both city and county folk.

Inside St Margaret's there has been every endeavour to keep pace with the times. In 1919 Mr William Howlett of Eastwood financed the installation of central heating in thanksgiving for the safe return of his three sons from the war. Electric lighting has been installed, as has carpeting; a public address system was installed in 1993 and, in 1998, a deaf-loop system. Even the organ, one of the integral parts of any church, has been upgraded. Samuel Gurney Buxton, in 1880, presented to St Margaret's an organ which was positioned next to the choir stalls and was manually pump operated (woe betide the boy chosen for this task if his attention wandered and the organ ran out of air). Leslie Potter was one of those who pumped away in the late thirties; "I also sang in the choir, which was better rewarded as each member was paid 1d per service and the whole choir had an annual outing to the seaside". It was not until just before World War II that a new electronic organ was purchased and was installed in the gallery which was then closed to the public. The gallery had in the past often been occupied by organised groups of younger parishioners; the teen-age boys of Mr Chevalier's army crammer were there each Sunday before the first World War and, subsequently, the village Girl Guides gathered there on Church Parade days. Maire Booty remembers them taking along pellets of paper which would be surreptitiously dropped onto the hats of those members of the congregation sitting directly beneath – Mrs Crampton's wide-brimmed hat was a favourite target. The prominent families in the village, like the Carters and the Woolseys, had their own pews in the nave of the church; the Buxton family always sat together in the pews near the choir, at right angles to the nave pews with their domestic staff and estate workers seated in the South Aisle.

The list of organists at St Margaret's includes such names as Mr Golding (reputedly 'as deaf as a post'), Mr Oldroyd and Donald Spinks, who played throughout the war years. But the one best remembered is Doreen Earl who took over from Mr Spinks in 1971 and continued for twenty two years until her retirement in 1993: she also gave piano lessons.

It was, in all likelihood, the presence of Catton Hall and the growing number of middle and upper class homes in the village during the nineteenth century that contributed to the dominance of the Church of England in Old Catton. There were no chapels there, unlike near neighbours Sprowston and Hellesdon each of which had, and still have, well-established non-conformist communities. But on the periphery of the village there were, for a time at least, two alternatives to the established church. On the North Walsham Road, close to Allens Lane, was a thriving Methodist Chapel run by the Futter family; Mr Futter ran the chapel, his wife looked after the social side, which included parties in her house for the local children, and their daughter Ethel played the organ in the chapel. This, however, closed down when the new Methodist Church was built on Wroxham Road and the building is now John Brown's funeral parlour, a sort of sequential change of use! On the south side of Old Catton, on Catton Grove Road, stood a small non-denominational chapel which has now been rebuilt as Wood Grove Chapel. There was also an out-post of St Margaret's in this area. A corrugated iron Church Mission Hall in Rackham Fields which had been built with money donated by the gentry of St Margaret's, and functioned for some years, but Sheila Barnby remembers it as being just an old tin hut where her Girl Guide company met in the 1930s – this survived until the 1960s when the local scouts demolished it and built their new headquarters on the site. By the end of the century Methodists were able to use the White Woman Lane school for Sunday worship and a small Pentecostal group met for a while in the Village Hall – until, that is, the neighbour complained of the noise of the enthusiastic singing!

But St Margaret's Church remained central to Old Catton life and provided for the spiritual needs of the great majority of its inhabitants. Until 1939 church activities were confined to the church itself and to the Parish Hall although there was a growing perception that a proper church hall was needed. This need became evident at the outbreak of World War II when the Parish Hall was turned into an army NAAFI. The Vicar, by this time the Revd Noel Boston, was conducting choir practices in the Vicarage because it was not possible to 'black-out' the Church and he now transferred other 'out of church' activities to a large shed in Mrs Currie's garden but soon found that this was not a satisfactory solution. So he acquired a piece of land in Attoe's Loke, just off St Clement's Hill, arranged for a nissen hut to be erected on it and named it St Margaret's Church Hall. Villagers remember this as a cosy meeting place but, unfortunately, it was not large enough for general use and declined into a Sunday School for young children, run by Miss Belton, a Religious Instruction teacher at the nearby Blyth School, and as a meeting place for the Guides. As things slowly got back to normal after the war, the Parish Hall was brought back into its proper use in 1946 and the corrugated Church Hall was sold and later demolished to make way for Carterford Drive.

So St Margaret's was still without a proper church hall and there was little prospect of gaining one until, in 1973, Mr Desmond Buxton gave sufficient land, during the development of Blacksmiths Way, to make one possible. There followed a fervent round of fund-raising by the village groups and individuals, including the children of the Sunday School who undertook a series of successful sponsored walks until, on Mothering Sunday, 25th March 1979, a brand new church hall was formally blessed and opened by the Bishop of Lynn. It has been in great demand ever since by church social groups and for occasional religious events such as the monthly Pram Service.

One difficulty that St Margaret's has faced has been the continual growth of the village on its northern side so that, geographically, it is no longer in a central position. In an effort to be more accessible to the many new villagers arrangements were made in the late 80s for monthly services to take place in the Scout Headquarters in Lodge Lane. This has proved a popular innovation and the services are usually conducted by the Revd Terry Patient who moved across to the ministry in 1996 upon his retirement from the teaching profession. It's a small world for Terry as the Scout Hall is alongside the school where he was for many years headmaster.

The churchyard was similarly faced with the problems associated with the growth of the village. It had been extended northwards in the latter part of the 19th Century but as the years went by it became increasingly obvious that it would be unable to cope with the growing population of the church's parish and, on 16th May, 1989, it was pronounced full and was closed. The Parish Council had been seeking land for a new cemetery and eventually bought a section of Mr

Ward's farm adjacent to the airfield and, on the 23rd of January, 1984, in a blinding snowstorm, this new cemetery was consecrated by the Bishop of Lynn, in the presence of Parish Councillors and church dignitaries of all denominations.

Finally, we must not overlook the Vicars who, each in their turn, took charge of church and parish, during the century. There were fourteen in total, some of them better remembered than others.

The Reverend Alan Dalby (1910–1917), for instance, was young and single when he took over and took up residence at the bottom end of Church Street. But in quick time he married and built the Vicarage on the corner of Fifers Lane for himself and his wife. He was responsible for having the ivy removed from the walls of St Margaret's and in so doing discovered the little statue of St Margaret in its niche above the porch.

The Revd David McCready (1934–1938) is remembered as a well built man with an imposing 'country gentleman' presence but he gained the attention of the small boys of the village by being the first Vicar to own a motor car. His wife attained a place in local history by jointly signing, with Mrs Rachel Buxton, all the copies of the New Testament that were given to the school children to commemorate King George VI's Coronation.

The Reverend Noel Boston (1939–1945) was the incumbent for precisely that period when memories were most acute. It fell to him to announce in church the outbreak of war and during that conflict he was immersed in all sorts of activities. He helped to organise stage entertainments in the Guide hut behind White House; he was persuaded to agree to exorcise a ghost that had been disturbing members of the ATS billeted in The Grange (however a German bomb dropped on the building and made any exorcism unnecessary). More rewarding for him was his foray to the bombed out church of St Benedict's in Norwich where he was able to retrieve organ pipes which were later installed in the gallery of St Margaret's and, of course, he was responsible for the setting up of the temporary church hall in Attoe's Loke. He was also renowned for his unusual hobbies, one of which was playing the Serpent (that antiquated wind instrument) and another was collecting ancient pistols. Mrs Wilby remembers that he took her and her new husband to the Vicarage immediately after the marriage ceremony to inspect his collection of pistols. She also recalls that the reception took place at the Samson and Hercules at a cost of £1 per head!

Canon Charles Howell, MBE (1970–1977), came from Tunstead where he had devoted much time and effort to renovating the old church. He seemingly welcomed such material challenges because one of his initiatives during his stay at St Margaret's was to lead a determined effort to retrieve the church-yard from the jungle it had become. He quickly recognised the need for a church hall, and when a suitable piece of land was offered he immersed himself in a vigorous programme of fund-raising. He was able to see the completion of the new Church Hall before he left the parish. However the most dedicated work took place in the foetid wartime prison camps of the Japanese where he did much to alleviate the suffering of his fellow prisoners. For this he was awarded the MBE.

The Revd Neil Mash (1977–1989) came from a theological training college in Canada, by way of parishes in Sussex, Suffolk and Swaffham, and as one of his first actions in the parish he was happy to plant a blue Atlas Cedar in the churchyard in commemoration of the Queen's Silver Jubilee. The Vicarage by this time was somewhat dilapidated and for the new Vicar and his wife Jean it was over-large and very cold, so it was with some relief that, just three years later, they learned that the Diocesan Authorities had decided to move them to a new and smaller Vicarage in Colkett Drive. They were even more delighted when the Diocese, after much hesitation, bought, in 1983, the present Vicarage which is ideally situated directly opposite to the church. By now there was a strong community spirit in the parish (it was renowned for its jumble sales held in the Village Hall each year and for its giant Guy Fawkes firework display on the field off St Faiths Road) and Neil Mash had little difficulty in starting a Men's Group for regular meetings and activities. On the distaff side his wife organised an expansion of the Mothers Union by forming an evening branch and, to embrace the up-and-coming generation, created a Young Wives Group. Unfortunately ill health forced him to retire in September 1989, and there followed an interregnum ably conducted by Mr George Latimer Williams, a Church Warden at St Margaret's for some twenty years.

The Revd Andrew Rayment came to St Margaret's in 1990 from the Earlham parish where he had enjoyed considerable success and was soon immersed in strengthening the presence of St Margaret's in the community. A new family service was introduced and, in October 1993, the Church Hall became the venue for the first of a series of monthly Pram Services, whilst the church was made more welcoming with new carpeting and a sound amplifying system. A link was established with the African community of Fiwila in Zambia. It was during this ministry that the Church of England strenuously debated the role of women in the church and, in 1995, Old Catton received its first woman curate, the Revd Helen Quinn, one of the first in Norfolk. It came as a shock to the parish when both priests resigned in November, 1996, for personal reasons. St Margaret's was plunged once more into an interregnum until the induction of the Revd Steven Betts on the 13th November, 1997, to see the parish into the new century.

EPILOGUE

Now, at the start of a new Millennium, we are a suburb of Norwich – "a very desirable suburb" according to the estate agents – but a vastly different place to that of 1950, let alone 1900!

We may wonder what was the most important event to contribute to the change over the century? Was it the coming of the buses in the 1930s, encouraging us to work and shop in the city? Was it the loss of the gentry at the outbreak of war in 1939, and later on of the other employment opportunities in the village, the brickyard, the farms, the smallholdings, causing the villagers to look further afield for work? Was it the loss of the squire in 1939, depriving the village of its de facto head and leader? Or was it the housing boom of 1950 and onwards that brought new faces but also 'commuters' wanting only somewhere to sleep and park the car? Could it have been the Norfolk Education Committee's decision to build additional schools in the village, thus separating the village so that half the children don't know the other half?

All these factors have played their part in the development of the village and there is now no readily identifiable focus of interest. The attractions of Norwich loom too large and many Old Catton people take no part in village activities, do not shop locally and spend most of their time and money in the city centre. There is less chance that they know their neighbours – a far cry from those pre-war years when children's transgressions were instantly recognised and quickly reported to the appropriate parents and when births, marriages and deaths were celebrated or mourned by all, rich and poor alike. But we should be satisfied that there is still a throb of activity in the Village Hall, the Church Hall, the Scout Headquarters and on the recreation grounds, and that the church, St Margaret's, continues to play its vibrant part in village life. Many of the old clubs and societies formed in the inter-war years still thrive – the Guides, Women's Institute, Mothers' Union, Royal British Legion, Horticultural Club – and the sports clubs, adult and junior, make full use of the recreation grounds. Since the last war new groups have been formed, such as the Scouts, Cubs and Brownies and, at the other end of the scale, the Old Friends Club. We even have a Meals on Wheels service and a Twinning Association with the village of Lavaré in France. And we have the Old Catton Society, formed at the same time as a Conservation Area was created in the village, to protect and preserve the village whenever possible and now gathering records, photographic and personal memories, to create an archive of village life.

And what of the future? The housing developments have filled the village, or it would seem so when the Lodge Farm development has been completed and the St Faiths Road allotments have been developed. But will houses eventually be built on Buttercup Meadow and the Parkland? Will Old Catton remain in the County or will it be swallowed up by Norwich? Only time will tell. Perhaps some village child of today will read this book in fifty years time and decide to update it. If so, we hope that he or she will get as much pleasure from the exercise as we have – pleasure of reminiscing with old friends, re-discovering facts and events of long ago, receiving the very willing co-operation of so many contributors.